Hands-On Science and Math

Fun, Fascinating Activities for Young Children

Beth R. Davis, EdS, NBCT

Dedication

This book is dedicated to the loving, compassionate, and hardworking staff of Kids For Kids Academy. Your dedication to finding the gifts and talents in every child and your sense of teamwork are to be admired. You truly make a difference every day with every child and family you touch.

Acknowledgments

A special thanks to Sandra Phillips, my volunteer lab assistant, whose commitment to inspiring young minds has made a difference for so many young children. Thanks for helping me to instill a love of science in our little scientists at Kids For Kids Academy!

Finally, my love goes out to my parents, Reva, Marty, Richard, and Marcia; my children, Rebekah and Benjamin; and my dearest friends, Julie, Diana, Kim, and Alina, for always believing in me. Your love, encouragement, and support made it possible for me to turn my dream of publishing this book into a reality.

GH10063
A Gryphon House Book

Hands-On Science and Math

Fun, Fascinating Activities for Young Children

Beth R. Davis, EdS, NBCT

Photography by Beth R. Davis

Gryphon House

Lewisville, NC

Copyright

Published by Gryphon House, Inc.

P.O. Box 10, Lewisville, NC 27023

800.638.0928; 877.638.7576 (fax)

Visit us on the web at www.gryphonhouse.com.

Cover photograph courtesy of Shutterstock Photography, ®2014, www.shutterstock.com.

Bulk Purchase

Gryphon House books are available for special premiums and sales promotions as well as for fund-raising use. Special editions or book excerpts also can be created to specifications. For details, contact the director of marketing at Gryphon House.

Disclaimer

Gryphon House, Inc., cannot be held responsible for damage, mishap, or injury incurred during the use of or because of activities in this book. Appropriate and reasonable caution and adult supervision of children involved in activities and corresponding to the age and capability of each child involved are recommended at all times. Do not leave children unattended at any time. Observe safety and caution at all times.

Library of Congress Cataloging-in-Publication Data

The Cataloging-in-Publication Data is registered with the Library of Congress for ISBN: 978-0-87659-649-4.

Table of Contents

Introduction

When children experience the joy of hands-on inquiry and discovery, math and science lessons really come to life. You have probably noticed that when youngsters learn by doing, they absorb the lessons in a lasting way. After a long day with the children, it is energizing when you see the lightbulb go off; you notice the excitement on their faces when they finally "get it" or make a new discovery.

The science and math activities contained in this book have been piloted and researched at Kids For Kids Academy in Miami, Florida, and have been successfully implemented in my school's early childhood science lab using inexpensive and easy-to-find materials. The key concepts are based on my experience as a National Board certified teacher and are modeled after research I conducted in the science lab and in my classroom over a seventeen-year period. The focus of each activity is pre-K to grade two, but teachers can vary and extend the activities for older children.

In my research, published by Florida International University (in a book edited by Jill Farrell and Robert Vos), I found that children exposed to hands-on science instruction gain greater subject-matter understanding than students exposed to only book learning or traditional worksheets. When I doubled the amount of hands-on instruction given to the lowest-performing student population in an at-risk class at a Florida elementary school, these children showed the highest gains when compared with ten other classes made up of average and above-average students in the same elementary school.

The activities contained in this book have been used at Kids For Kids Academy preschool since 2006. Most of the voluntary pre-K students enrolled and exposed to these hands-on science activities have entered kindergarten prepared for success. Since its inception, Kids For Kids Academy students have achieved readiness ratings in the top 10 percent of preschool students in Miami–Dade County, Florida. These students are exposed to activities that foster critical thinking while they are participating in hands-on scientific inquiry not only in the school science lab, but also in other classes as teachers infuse science and math seamlessly throughout the school day.

On the pages that follow, you will find research-based methods, detailed explanations of science concepts and discussions, as well as step-by-step directions for hands-on science activities. On gryphonhouse.com, you can view videos of these activities done with preschoolers in my early childhood science lab. The videos show the instruction as well as how the children interact with the materials.

Mathematical thinking and scientific discovery are great opportunities to develop critical thinking skills in young children. To do this, children must be conscious of the world around them by exploring using their senses: touch, sound, sight, taste, and smell. Activities such as nature walks, visits to a school garden, and hands-on science explorations allow children to touch nature, see bugs, and listen to outdoor sounds.

Children can count the types of animals they see and make comparisons with regard to sizes, colors, shapes, and environments. Foster the children's inquiry skills by providing science and other materials that allow for exploration throughout the classroom, not solely in discovery areas. Include items such as

- books with various textures;
- instruments that make different sounds;
- music;
- water and sand play;
- playdough to form shapes and compare colors;
- floor mats with various textures to learn to take apart, touch, and put together;
- opportunities for painting with fingers and brushes;
- learning to paste objects; and
- touching and feeling different textures.

Observations and opportunities for discovery can also take place in school gardens, where children can plant seeds or seedlings, water their plants, and make observations about growth. When the plants are grown, children can pick and eat the foods. Using plants and animals as well as manipulatives, children can count, sort, and classify to reinforce mathematical thinking.

Scientific thinking enables children to gain an understanding of the world in which they live. Encourage them to ask questions and use simple tools as they make comparisons. As we respond to youngsters, answer their questions, and show examples, we can help develop their ability to draw conclusions from observations. The activities contained in this book provide opportunities for young children to experience science and math in a way that is meaningful and promotes critical thinking and problem solving.

Learning
and Experimenting

Young children are filled with wonder and excitement. They are hungry for science and are easily amazed. Even when we challenge them to stretch and explore concepts that some might feel are too abstract, we give them opportunities to grasp bits and pieces of the ideas. By repeating the same activity from year to year, each time the children are exposed to the experience, they absorb greater levels of understanding of the same concept. In addition to exposing preschoolers and early learners to hands-on science, allow them to engage in free exploration. Through unstructured exploration, we foster the development of imagination and creativity.

Practical Tips for Science Explorations

In general, stick with concepts that are basic and not too abstract. Remember that these are preschoolers! While executing science experiments, it is best to work in small groups. It helps to give each child a tray to manage materials and define personal space. You can purchase plastic trays from a dollar store or ask a local grocery store to donate unused foam meat trays that you can reuse many times.

To be most effective, infuse your daily routines with science inquiry. Science can be easily integrated throughout your day. Provide opportunities for children to visit, play, and learn

SAFETY FIRST!

Safety is an important concept to introduce when teaching science. When you set these expectations, the children maintain better focus and concentration on the concepts being presented. Go over lab safety rules each time children participate in science experiments—for example:

- Leave all belongings outside the lab area.
- No running in the lab; always walk to avoid accidents.
- No shouting or playing around.
- When coming to the lab table, all hands should go under the table until the teacher gives instructions otherwise.
- Wear safety goggles to protect your eyes if you are working with chemicals or vinegar.
- Tie back long hair.
- No food or drink in the lab unless it is part of the experiment.
- Never smell or taste anything unless the teacher tells you to do so.
- Listen and follow all instructions carefully.
- Ask questions if you are uncertain about what to do during the experiment.
- Wash your hands with soap before and after touching animals.
- When you have completed an experiment, put waste materials in the correct containers.

in their science and discovery center, and stock the center with numerous activities and materials for children to observe and explore:

- Microscopes
- Hand lenses
- Rock and shell samples
- Sensory bottles and tables
- Magnets
- Real and plastic insects
- X-rays
- Variety of items to sort

Additional items can be rotated in and out of the center. When planning activities and stocking the classroom with exploration materials, provide a variety of options. Consider using recycled items to cut down on cost while also teaching the children how to reuse and be kind to our planet. You might have animals in the classroom that the children can observe daily. Stock class libraries, discovery areas, and the school library with books based on various science themes. Create a garden with plants to water, observe, and harvest. You might want to schedule cooking activities regularly to practice science process skills, math, and following directions. You can align weekly science experiments with themes being taught each week and then provide opportunities for free exploration related to the themes.

Doing What Scientists Do

You can accomplish preschool science goals by practicing what scientists do:

- Observe objects, events, and people.
- Find words to describe observations and to communicate ideas.
- Ask questions.
- Explore and investigate to try to answer questions.
- Use science tools to observe and measure.
- Record observations using simple drawings and basic charts.

Use science process skills as a framework to guide scientific inquiry in the early childhood setting: observe, measure, classify, predict, experiment, and communicate.

By familiarizing younger children with the science process skills, you help prepare them for the transition to the scientific method, which is introduced in the early elementary grades.

SCIENCE PROCESS SKILLS

- Observe
- Measure
- Classify
- Predict
- Experiment
- Communicate

Math and Science Go Hand in Hand

Once the children have begun to develop their science process skills, they will be inclined to ask more questions that foster higher levels of critical thinking. Mathematical thinking and scientific discovery go hand in hand. Look for opportunities to link the two by having children follow step-by-step directions, count, measure, and interpret data during explorations. Involving children in meaningful experiences allows them to observe the world around them, think scientifically, and solve problems in a mathematical way.

A Closer Look with the Hand Lens

CONCEPTS

As you teach children the role of a scientist, be sure that they understand the proper use of the tools that scientists use. In this activity, children learn the use of a hand lens as a tool for making things appear bigger.

DISCUSSION

A scientist is someone who studies something to learn more about it. Scientists use special tools as they explore new things. Sometimes, scientists want to get a closer look at something to see all the little details. A hand lens, also called a magnifier, helps by making small things bigger and easier to see. To use a hand lens, the children should hold it in one hand and close one eye. Sometimes it is easier for a small child to cover one eye. The child should place the hand lens near one eye and look through it. He can place the item he is looking at in his other hand or on the table. Sometimes, it helps to put the item on top of an upside-down cup. That way, the child can get a closer look by using one hand to cover one eye and the other to hold the hand lens.

MATERIALS

For each child:
- Small tray
- Unbreakable hand lens
- Variety of items to examine, such as pennies, stamps, flowers, rocks, shells, and tree-trunk pieces

ACTIVITY

1. Place several small items on a plate or on a tray. Call out the name of each item one at a time, and have the children pick up the item and look at it using the magnifier. With older children, you can include some items with tiny print such as stamps or pennies. Discuss whether the magnifier made each item bigger or smaller.

2. After looking at several items, give each child rocks, shells, tree-trunk pieces, and other items found in nature, and instruct them to take a closer look at each one.

3. Encourage the children to get a closer look at their hands. Have them explain what looks different about their hands when viewing them with the hand lenses versus without the lenses.

4. Go on a scavenger hunt. Give each child a hand lens, and instruct the children to find tiny things in their environment and to use a hand lens to magnify those items.

MINDING THE MATH

Have the children draw an outline of one of the objects. Have them look at the object with the hand lens and then draw a larger outline around the original one to estimate how much bigger the object looks when magnified. This activity will visually reinforce for the concept of magnification and the degree of enlargement.

LITERACY EXTENSION

Have each child craft a language experience story about what happened when she drank magic shrinking juice and became so tiny that she could be seen only with a hand lens. Prewriters can dictate their stories to the teacher, and writers can write down their own stories.

Pouring and More: Funnels and Test Tubes

CONCEPTS

You will introduce the funnel as a tool scientists and other individuals use to prevent spills. Once children know how to use a funnel, you can add it to the sand-and-water table. You will also introduce test tubes as tools for holding liquids. The children will explore the proper use of test tubes and the use of funnels to make pouring easier.

DISCUSSION

Sometimes we want to pour something into a container with a small opening. A funnel makes it easier to pour liquids into small spaces without spilling. A scientist uses test tubes to study liquids and other small items. Test tubes are slender containers that hold liquid. To use a funnel, simply place the small end of the funnel into the test tube or container you wish to fill. Then, pour the water into the big opening of the funnel, and the water will flow into the container.

ACTIVITY

1. Give each child a test-tube rack. Instruct the children to place their test tubes inside the plastic containers to be used as catch basins. Each child will also need another container filled with water and a small cup. If you use colored water, the children will find the activity more interesting and easier to see.

2. Demonstrate by putting a funnel into the first test tube in a rack. Hold the test tube in the air, and show the children the top and bottom of the test tube or little water bottle. Using a cup, scoop some water from the

MATERIALS

- Food coloring (optional)
- Variety of containers
- Cups in a variety of sizes
- Small portion cups (available at dollar, party, and restaurant-supply stores)

For each child:
- Funnel
- Test-tube rack and plastic test tubes (Note: You can use 8-ounce water bottles as an alternative.)
- Plastic container large enough to hold a test-tube rack
- Plastic container filled with water
- Cup

plastic water-filled container. Ask the children to tell you when the water poured into the funnel reaches the top of the test tube or bottle. Slowly begin pouring, and stop when the children tell you to stop.

3. When the first test tube is filled, demonstrate moving the funnel from one test tube to the next. Practice filling the other test tubes and letting the children tell you when the water reaches the top of each one.

4. Give the children a chance to practice pouring the water into their own test tubes or water bottles. It will be easier for smaller children to do this standing up.

5. Once the children know how to use funnels, you can leave funnels in the sand-and-water or sensory tables along with various containers for practice and free exploration.

MINDING THE MATH

Give each child a small portion cup, and ask the children to predict how many tiny cups it will take to fill a test tube or other small container. The children can say their predictions out loud, write them on the board, or write them on sticky notes. If you use sticky notes, you can arrange the predictions from smallest to largest. You can vary the size of the cup, such as using tiny coffee-shot cups or small bathroom drinking cups, to vary the experience. Count how many cups it will take to fill various containers. Older children can create a graph showing their findings or a graph showing their predictions.

LITERACY EXTENSION

Write the word *funnel* on the board. Break the word down into syllables. Have the children clap their hands for each syllable. Count the number of letters in the word, and discuss the beginning sound. Ask if there are any letters repeated in the word. Point out that the letter *n* appears twice in the word, if they do not notice.

Tools for Drips and Drops

CONCEPTS

The children will become familiar with the proper way to use pipettes or droppers for experiments involving liquids. Teaching children to squeeze and release the dropper is great for improving small-motor muscles. The pipette can also be used to discuss the concept of air: When the pipette is squeezed, the air is pushed out. When it is let go, the air outside the dropper pushes the water inside the dropper.

DISCUSSION

Tell the children that pipettes, also called droppers, are used to measure and pick up small amounts of liquids. When you need to take a little bit of medicine, the person who takes care of you can use a dropper to measure and give you just the right amount. Air is all around us, including inside a pipette. The top of a pipette is called a bulb. When you squeeze the bulb, you push the air out of the pipette. When you place the dropper in the water and let go of the bulb, air pressure around you will push the water inside the pipette. By squeezing the bulb again, the water is pushed out.

ACTIVITY

1. Demonstrate the procedure by squeezing the bulb end of the pipette. This pushes the air out of the dropper. With the bulb squeezed, place the other end of the dropper in the water. With the end of the pipette in the water, let go of the bulb so that it is no longer squeezed. Air pressure will push the water into the dropper.

2. Remove the dropper from the water, and squeeze the bulb over the empty container to let the water out.

3. Give each child a dropper or pipette, a small container of water, and something to transfer the water into. For younger children, use bigger containers for catching the water; egg cartons work well. For older children, water-bottle lids or film canisters (available through science-supply stores) work well. You can also ask a pharmacy to donate unused pill blister packs, which have very small spaces for storing pills. Children with good motor control can easily squeeze water into these blister packs. They will also love transferring the water from one hole to another.

4. Have the children practice taking in the water and squeezing it out into the containers. This exercise helps improve fine-motor skills.

MINDING THE MATH

Have the children predict how many pipettes full of water they will need to fill a plastic lid. Count as each dropper is filled and emptied into the plastic lid. Compare their predictions with the actual experiment results.

Water Sense and Cents: Surface Tension

CONCEPTS

Water is made up of tiny molecules. Each one is like a little magnet. At the edges of each drop of water, the molecules line up like little minimagnets, attaching to each other. They form a kind of skin on top of the drop, holding the rest of the water in. The "skin" is called *surface tension*. When there is too much water on the skin, the surface tension breaks and the water will overflow.

In this activity, the children will predict how many drops of water can fit on a penny. They will do the same for other coins and then graph the results.

ACTIVITY

1. Hold up a penny and wonder aloud, "How much water do you think a penny could hold on its surface?" With the children, determine the problem statement: How many drops of water will a penny hold?
2. Ask each child to make a hypothesis or guess: How many drops do you predict the penny will hold?
3. Create a data table on a piece of paper or on the whiteboard. In a T chart, list penny, nickel, dime, and quarter in the left-hand column. The right-hand column is where you will record the number of drops each type of coin can hold.
4. Place a penny with the head side up on a paper towel. (Using the same side of the penny eliminates the variable of the different crevices.)
5. Fill a dropper with water.
6. Drop the water one drop at time on the penny, and count how many drops the penny holds.

MATERIALS

For each child:
- Pipette
- Penny
- Paper towel
- Small container of water

- Nickels, dimes, and quarters to share
- Paper or whiteboard
- Marker

7. When the surface tension breaks, record on the data table how many drops the penny held.

8. Repeat the experiment for the other coins.

HOW MANY DROPS OF WATER FIT ON THE HEAD OF A COIN?	
Coin	Number of Drops
Penny	
Nickel	
Dime	
Quarter	

9. Summarize your results using the data from the table:

The penny held _____ drops of water.

The nickel held _____ drops of water.

The dime held _____ drops of water.

The quarter held _____ drops of water.

MINDING THE MATH

Create a bar graph of your results, and let the children help fill in the boxes. The graph provides visual support for the math concepts, so count the shaded boxes in each column with the children. Ask questions such as which has more and which has fewer.

DROPS OF WATER THAT FIT ON EACH COIN

Number of Drops		Penny	Nickel	Dime	Quarter
	20				
	19				
	18				
	17				
	16				
	15				
	14				
	13				
	12				
	11				
	10				
	9				
	8				
	7				
	6				
	5				
	4				
	3				
	2				
	1				

Hands-On Science and Math

Sink or Float

CONCEPTS

This activity offers so many learning opportunities. In addition to sinking and floating, the children can explore scooping, pouring, dumping, liquids, counting, comparing, the sense of touch, wet and dry, making predictions, drawing conclusions, opposites, cold, empty, full, round, square, the letters *f* and *s* and their sounds, and following directions.

DISCUSSION

Begin by asking the children if they know some things that water is used for. Some answers may include drinking, swimming, taking a bath, or making rain. Some children may say there is water in the ocean. If they do not offer these ideas, find a way to bring them into the conversation. Discuss the importance of knowing that they should never go into a pool or other body of water alone. Continue the discussion by asking if they know how to float on top of the water. Explain that the word *float* means to stay on top of the water. Ask if any of the children have ever floated in a pool. Next, discuss that sinking is the opposite of floating. Something that sinks falls to the bottom of a container of water.

ACTIVITY

1. Place a cork in a clear, empty container. Slowly pour water into the container, and have the children observe.
2. Note that as the water is poured, the cork will stay on top of the water. Discuss that the cork is floating in the container.

3. Do the same demonstration with a marble or metal object, and discuss that when water is poured on one of those items, the item stays on the bottom or sinks.

4. Let each child drop a penny in the clear container so that she can see the penny sinking to the bottom. Compare sinking to floating.

5. Instruct the children to put their hands in the water, and ask them how it feels. (Of course, it is wet and probably cold.) Give them an opportunity to explore the water with their hands.

6. To continue the activity, pick up the metal washer, and tell the children what it is. Ask them what shape it is. Then ask, "What do you think will happen if I drop it in the water?" Allow the children time to make predictions. Count the number of children who predict the washer will sink and who predict it will float.

7. Have the children watch what happens when the washer is dropped into the container of water. Ask if it sank to the bottom of the water or floated on top. Continue to review that something that sinks will fall to the bottom and that something that floats will stay on the top.

8. Before trying the next item, have the children predict or guess whether the item will sink or float. Continue guessing and testing their predictions with each item. Be sure to engage in discussion about each item to expand the children's vocabulary. Discuss the physical properties such as the sizes, shapes, and colors of the items.

9. Fishing the items out of the water is just as much fun as putting them in. Instruct the children to put their hands under the table. This will give them a chance to focus on what you are saying as you guide the next part of the activity.

10. Point out the two empty bowls and the words *sink* and *float* that appear on the bowls. Discuss the meaning of each word, and ask the children to name the first letters of the words *sink* and *float.*

11. Name one of the items that you tested. Ask the children to look in their containers of water and tell you whether that item floated or sank. Instruct them to fish out that item with their hands, and model placing the item in the bowl that corresponds with whether the item sank or floated. Continue calling out items as the children put the items in corresponding bowls.

MINDING THE MATH

1. Once each of the items is in a bowl, remove the container of water (to eliminate the distraction) and show your bowl labeled *sink*. One by one, take out the items and line them up on the table. As you touch each item, have the children count out loud each item you touch.

2. Continue by counting the items in the bowl labeled *float*.

3. On a piece of paper, create a Buoyancy Graph that the children can help fill in.

BUOYANCY GRAPH

Number of Items		Floated	Sank
	7		
	6		
	5		
	4		
	3		
	2		
	1		
		Floated	**Sank**
		What happened?	

4. Review how many items sank and floated, and have the children help color in the boxes on the chart or tape paper squares in each box to represent the items. The graph provides visual support for the math concepts, so have the children count the boxes shaded in each column. Ask questions such as which has more and which has fewer.

5. Another graphing option is a picture graph. Take photos of each item, and place the photos in the boxes that correspond with what happened to the item when it was dropped in water.

Buoyancy and Salt Water

CONCEPTS

This activity is suitable for older children and extends some of the concepts in the Sink or Float activity. When salt is added to water, it increases the water's density. This means that it is easier for items placed in salt water to float or remain buoyant.

DISCUSSION

The more salt in water, the easier it is for objects to float on the water. It is easier to float in oceans containing salt water than in fresh water. Divers often wear heavy belts to keep from floating to the ocean surface. When a hard-boiled egg is placed in salt water, the salt water is denser than the egg, and the egg floats.

MATERIALS

- Water
- Salt
- Hard-boiled egg
- Large cup or container
- Spoon
- Paper
- Markers, pencils, or crayons

ACTIVITY

1. Hold up a hard-boiled egg, and ask the children whether or not it will float in water. Place the egg in a cup of plain water, and watch as it sinks to the bottom. Scoop the egg out, and ask the children what is needed to help the egg float in the water. If they do not say salt, lead them to that idea.

2. Discuss the problem statement for this activity: How many tablespoons of salt will it take to float an egg?

3. Ask each child to come up with a hypothesis or guess: How many tablespoons will it take to float the egg? Record their guesses on a piece of paper or on the board.

4. Place the hard-boiled egg in an empty container, and fill the container with water.

5. Stir in 1 tablespoon of salt, and observe what happens.
6. Continue adding tablespoons of salt, one at a time, until the egg floats.
7. Ask the children to report how many tablespoons of salt it took to float the egg.
8. To get the children thinking about the results, ask them to draw the cup with the egg before the salt was added. Then, ask them draw the cup with the egg after the salt was added.
9. Discuss the differences.

MINDING THE MATH

Following the activity, review the number of tablespoons it took to float the egg. Measure out the same number of tablespoons, but place them in a measuring cup to see what portion of the cup they fill—¼, ½, or 1 cup.

LITERACY EXTENSION

Brainstorm activities the children like to do when they play in water. List their ideas on the board, and write a language experience story together. Have each child copy down a sentence and illustrate it. Older children can write their own stories.

Magnetic Attraction

CONCEPTS

The children will learn about magnetism and then will examine and test a variety of items to see if they are magnetic. Next, they will sort the items into categories by whether or not they are magnetic. Finally, they will count and graph the number of items that were attracted to a magnet and the number of items not attracted to a magnet. Other concepts discussed are letter sounds and the words *yes* and *no*.

DISCUSSION

Tell the children that a magnet attracts (brings near) things that are made of certain metals. Items that are not magnetic will not stick to the magnet. Point out that they will have a tray with different items and three empty bowls. Explain that the bowls are marked with *n-o,* which spells the word *no,* and *y-e-s,* which spells the word *yes.* Tell the children that they will test items to see if they will stick to or be attracted to a magnet. If the item is attracted, it will go in the *yes* bowl. If not, it will be placed in the *no* bowl. The bowl labeled *I don't know* is where items will be placed for testing.

MATERIALS

For each child:
- Tray
- Wand magnet
- Variety of items to test, such as wood, plastic, metal, rubber, and magnetic marbles
- Bowl labeled *I don't know*
- Bowl labeled *yes*
- Bowl labeled *no*

ACTIVITY

1. Give each child a tray with the three bowls, the items to be tested, and a magnet. Have the children keep their hands under the table so they will not be inclined to touch everything on the tray. Remind them of the uses for the three bowls, and review the words *yes* and *no.*

2. Ask them to pick up something made of rubber, such as a rubber stopper, eraser, or rubber band, and place it in the I don't know bowl.

3. Have them pick up the magnet wand in one hand and demonstrate testing the first item. As you and the children touch your magnets to the rubber items, ask if the rubber item sticks to the magnet. Direct them to move the item from the I don't know bowl to the no bowl.

4. Next choose an item that will be attracted to the magnet, such as a metal washer or paper clip. Ask the children to pick up the item and place it in the I don't know bowl. Ask them to touch their magnet wand to the item. Ask if the item sticks to the magnet. When they say yes, have them pick up the item and put it in the yes bowl.

5. Continue to let the children test the items one at a time. Make predictions or guesses before testing each item.

MINDING THE MATH

When the children are finished testing the items, instruct them to take the items that were attracted to the magnet out of the yes bowl and line them up in front of them. Line up your items as well. Move your finger from one item to the next, and ask the children to help you count how many items were attracted to the magnet. Repeat this process for the items in the no bowl. You can also make a graph depicting the number of yes and no responses. Discuss which category has more items, the yes category or the no category. You can even do simple math and count the total number of items tested.

MAGNET GRAPH

Number of Items		Magnetic	Not Magnetic
	6		
	5		
	4		
	3		
	2		
	1		
		What Happened?	

Map the Magnetic Poles

CONCEPTS

In this activity the children will learn about the concepts of attract and repel. They will use a compass to find the north and south poles of the magnet and will investigate to find out that like poles repel and opposite poles attract.

MATERIALS

- Bar or horseshoe magnet for each child
- Several compasses to share
- Masking tape or colored sticky dots
- Pencils
- Globe

DISCUSSION

While holding the globe, point out the north and south poles. Explain that the earth has magnetic properties and that a compass aligns itself on the north and south poles of the earth's magnet. Show the compass, and point out the letters *N, S, E,* and *W,* explaining that those letters stand for north, south, east, and west. Walk outside, and change your direction as you walk so the children can see the needle on the compass moving. When you are back inside, show a magnet. Explain that the magnet also has a north and south pole.

ACTIVITY

1. Hold one side of the magnet to the compass, and see in which direction the needle on the compass is pointing. Then, try the other side of the magnet, so the children can see the needle move.
2. Write S and N on pieces of masking tape or on sticky dots, and let the children stick them on the appropriate poles of their magnets. Some magnets may have the poles already marked.
3. Once they have marked both poles of the magnets, explain that like poles will repel, or push away from, each other. Write the word *repel* on the board, and

discuss that it starts with the letter *r*. This means a south pole of one magnet will push away a south pole of another magnet. Poles that are different or opposite will attract or come together. Write the word *attract* and point out the first letter of the word.

4. Give the children a chance to practice making their magnets attract and repel. To make it very visual, put one magnet on the table and push it away using the like pole of another magnet.

MINDING THE MATH

On the board, draw the cardinal points of the compass with intersecting arrows and labels: north, south, east, and west. Have the children count how many directions are listed.

Chapter

2

Measuring, Identifying, and Classifying

Number sense and mathematical thinking are critical parts of early development and of science. Through varied explorations and experiences, children can gain an understanding of counting; sorting; organizing sets; comparing, recognizing, and manipulating shapes; and using concrete objects. They can learn to explain the world through positional words; to measure and compare quantities, length, height, and weight; and to analyze data. By participating in daily calendar activities, children can count up to thirty-one and understand the pattern of adding one. They learn ordinal position and reinforce it daily when lining up—who is first, second, third, and so on. Playing with counting bears, children compare sets by combining (more) and taking away (fewer) while also learning pattern recognition and duplicating.

There are so many ways to encourage the children to develop their math skills:

- Compare—Which group has more, and which has fewer items?
- Describe objects—Create an animal graph of school pets, organized by characteristics such as furry, scaly, feathered, and smooth.
- Understand two-dimensional shapes—Search for circles, squares, and triangles.
- Use positional words—Let them show you under, over, below, above, and next.

Give them opportunities to sing counting songs and to sort and classify items by size, color, and so on. Integrate mathematical thinking whenever possible as you teach science concepts.

Get the Picture through Graphing

Graphing activities help develop number sense and strategies for counting, comparing, and keeping track of quantities. Graphing also teaches children to collect, record, and represent data in a variety of organized ways. A bar graph compares data via the length of the bars, which may be horizontal or vertical. A pictograph represents data in pictures. Tallying activities help develop strategies for one-to-one correspondence, counting, and recording mathematical information, which aid in the development of number and operation sense.

Use graphing to encourage critical-thinking skills, language development, self-expression, and math skills. At the beginning of the school year, give each child a 2-inch-square card with his photo and name on it. If you laminate it, the card will last all year long. Teach the children that the cards with their photos will be used to represent their votes each time the class answers a graphing question. If you make this a part of your daily routine, you can use it as a classroom management strategy. In my elementary classroom, I had each child pick up his photo card on the way in and place it in the box next to his corresponding vote on the way to his seat. If a card was left behind, it told me that the child was absent from school (or had forgotten to vote). In a preschool classroom, the children can pick up their cards by identifying their names and photos. Present the graphing topic to the children in circle time, and have each child place his picture card in the space that represents his vote among the choices presented. After the children cast their votes, guide them to count how many of each choice is represented by the photo cards in each category. The children can discuss and compare which item has more or fewer votes, providing opportunities for data interpretation. Potential graphing topics are listed in the Appendix.

A Slice of Life: Tree-Trunk Explorations

CONCEPTS

Children will use their sense of smell to sniff cross sections of evergreen trees. You can use donated Christmas trees, with trunks cut into 1- to 2-inch sections, or you can buy the tree blocks online. The children will put things in order from smallest to largest, use a hand lens to get a closer look at the rings of the trees, and use a tape measure to determine the distance across tree blocks and the height of their structures. The concept of recycling can also be introduced in this lesson.

DISCUSSION

Explain that you are going to be working with something that is recycled, which means that it is used in a new way instead of throwing it away. Ask each child to smell a tree block. Ask them what it smells like. Tell them that the block was once a Christmas tree and that previously it was a pine tree growing in the ground. Before beginning the lesson, review the proper use of a hand lens, and have each child look at the block with his hand lens and point out the rings. Count the rings and explain that the rings tell us how old the tree was before it was cut down.

MATERIALS

For each child and the teacher:

- Container
- 10 tree blocks (1- or 2-inch-thick cross sections)
- Hand lens
- Tape measure or ruler
- Paper clips or snapping cubes (optional)

ACTIVITY

1. Give each child a container of ten blocks, a hand lens, and a tape measure or ruler.
2. Using your own set, demonstrate how to put the blocks in order from smallest to largest. Instruct the children to put their blocks in that order.

3. Count the blocks. For younger children, touch each block with your finger as they count, assisting them with one-to-one correspondence.

4. Using a tape measure or ruler, show the children how to measure across the block. Younger children can use paper clips or snapping cubes as a means of nonstandard measure.

5. Instruct the children to build a tower, making sure that the largest block is on the bottom and the smallest block is on the top. You can also put the tree-trunk slices in your block area and give the children opportunities to use them for building and free exploration.

MINDING THE MATH

Older children can use a tape measure to measure the height of their block-tower structures. Younger children can measure their towers using nonstandard measures such as hands or lengths of yarn. You can also put the blocks on a scale and weigh them, recording the weight of each block. Children can graph the size of their block towers in inches, centimeters, or using nonstandard measures.

TREE-BLOCK GRAPH

Number of Inches		Block 1	Block 2	Block 3	Block 4	Block 5	Block 6	Block 7	Block 8	Block 9	Block 10
	8										
	7										
	6										
	5										
	4										
	3										
	2										
	1										

Blocks

LITERACY EXTENSION

Discuss the many uses for trees, and write them on the board. Assist the children in writing a language experience story about how trees help us to live.

Another option is to have the children sit under a tree and write a story about their favorite kind of tree. One child might recount a memory related to a Christmas tree, and another might write about a tree that grows his favorite fruit.

Lots of Lids

The children will sort, count, graph, and make comparisons with a variety of lids. My nickname for this lesson is "Making Something Out of Nothing at All." Accumulating huge lid collections is easy. Simply put a box somewhere in the school, and ask families to recycle by bringing in used lids. You will find that the children tend to play with these items more than commercial toys.

MATERIALS

- 2 large containers
- Assortment of plastic lids in a variety of colors
- Index cards
- Markers
- Tray for each child

DISCUSSION

Scientists classify items to make it easier to study topics. For example, doctors specialize in the branch of medicine that they study and practice. When you want to have your teeth checked, you go to a dentist. When you need to have your eyes checked, you go to an optometrist or ophthalmologist. In this activity, the children will begin to practice their sorting skills.

ACTIVITY

1. Play a sorting game, and divide the children into two groups. Calling the children by name, put all of the boys in one group and all of the girls into another. Ask the children to figure out how the groups were sorted.

2. Continue the game, and this time sort the children by shirt color or hair length. As they become better critical thinkers, you can make the sorting criteria harder to figure out, such as sorting by shoe type (laces or not) or other attributes.

3. Explain to the children that they are going to sort lids by color. Give each child a tray with one colored lid on it (different colors for different children). Have the rest of the lids nearby in two big containers.

4. Divide the children up around the two containers. Ask them to look through the containers to find lids of the same color as the lids they have on their trays. Each child should collect lids of his color on his tray; they can also work in pairs. After a child has picked out the lids from one container, he can switch containers and look for his color in the second container. For crowd control, this works better than just spilling out all the lids on the floor.

5. In a big open space, have each child take her tray to a spot on the floor and line up her lids in one row. Then, have each child count how many lids are in her row. Assist younger children as needed.

6. Have the children lie down next to their rows to see if they are shorter or taller than their rows of lids.

MINDING THE MATH

Let each child point to the lids in his row as his classmates count how many are in the row. Determine by counting and by visual representation which rows have the most and fewest lids.

LITERACY EXTENSION

When the lids are lined up, have the children help you write the color words on index cards to mark each color row. If you are only sorting the lids onto the trays, the word cards can be used to label the trays. Use the corresponding color of crayon or ink when writing the words. For younger children, ask them to draw a picture to represent the color, such as a purple circle for purple lids or a red circle for red lids. Write the corresponding color word alongside the drawing.

What Sort Is It?

CONCEPTS

Children love to sort just about anything! In this activity, they will learn how to classify and group items by size, color, shape, and other characteristics. Sorting can be done for free exploration or as part of a structured activity. It is easy to collect materials for sorting. Simply let parents know what you are collecting, and provide an area for them to drop off donated items.

DISCUSSION

All kinds of recycled items can be sorted and classified according to different characteristics. When you have a good assortment of items in your collection box, discuss with the children what you are going to sort, and ask them to suggest ways the items could be sorted. Consider and discuss the following possibilities.

- Stamps: Sort by living and nonliving subjects, people and animals, numbers and letters, or types of objects.
- Hardware: Sort nuts and bolts by size or shape.
- Pattern-block shapes: Sort by shape, size, or color.
- Keys: Some hardware stores will throw away keys made as mistakes. See if they will donate. Sort keys by color, size, shape, type, or shape of the hole.
- Paper clips: Sort by plastic versus metal, striped or solid, color, or size.
- Bread tags: Sort by size, shape, color, or those with words and those with numbers.
- Buttons: Sort by size, shape, color, number of holes, plastic, or metal.
- Bottle caps: Sort by color and type.
- Barrettes: Sort by color, shape, and size.

MATERIALS

- Paper
- Marker

For each child:
- Egg carton, bowls, or sorting mat
- Variety of items to be sorted, such as buttons, keys, plastic lids, barrettes, pattern blocks, stamps, nuts, bolts, and washers

■ Lids: Sort by size, shape, color, metal or plastic, lids that pop or lids that do not, and lids that have print on the top or lids that do not.

ACTIVITY

1. Create a sorting mat for each child by drawing a large circle in the middle of a piece of paper. Next draw six circles on the outside of the large circle so the drawing looks like a flower. The sorting mat can be used to establish personal space and to assist in the sorting process. See the graphic for examples of sorting mats. You might want to have a four-item sorting template on one side of the mat and a larger number of categories on the other side. If you laminate the sorting mats, then they can be used year after year. You can also use small paper plates or little bowls. Place one in the middle for the items to be sorted, and arrange the others around it. Another option is to recycle an egg carton for sorting.
2. Have each child begin the sorting process by choosing a group of items and placing the items in the center section of her sorting mat.
3. Ask the children to sort the items on their mats into groups by certain characteristics, putting them into the outer shapes on the mat. (Choose the side of the mat with more or fewer sorting circles, depending on the task.)
4. After sorting the items, the children should place them back in the container.
5. Then, each child can choose another container to sort.

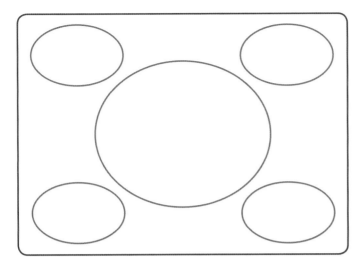

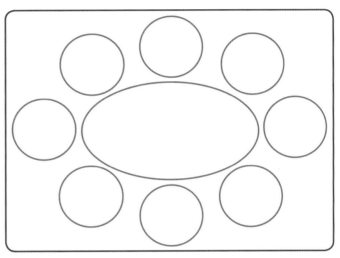

Items to be sorted go in the center of the mat, and children can use the outer shapes for sorting the items into categories.

MINDING THE MATH

When a child has sorted a container of items by an attribute, such as color, ask the child to count the number of items in each category. For younger children, point to each item as you count together, reinforcing one-to-one correspondence.

Classifying Liquids and Solids

CONCEPTS

The children will learn to identify solids and liquids. Through exploration they will deepen their understanding of texture, measuring, and pouring. As part of their learning, they will increase their vocabulary and recognize letter sounds.

MATERIALS

- Tray
- Empty clear cup
- Rock
- Plastic lid
- Variety of solid objects, such as nuts, bolts, washers, blocks, and marbles
- Variety of liquids, such as milk, juice, water, and soda
- Chart paper or whiteboard
- Marker
- Camera (optional)
- Old magazines
- Scissors
- Tape

DISCUSSION

Write the words *liquid* and *solid* large enough for all the children to see. Point to each word as you pronounce it, and discuss what letter the word starts with. In very simple terms, explain that liquids are things that are wet and can be poured. Demonstrate by pouring water into a cup and asking if it is wet and can be poured. Let the children feel the water to gain an understanding that it is wet. Continue by pouring each of the liquids into different cups and asking each time:

- Does it pour?
- Is it a liquid?

After the children have an understanding of liquids, explain that solids are different from liquids. A solid is hard and cannot pour. To demonstrate, you can pick up the rock, bang it on the table, and ask, "Can you pour a rock?" For effect, hold a cup under the rock, and try to pour the rock. Do the same for the other solids on your demonstration tray. Alternate between liquids and solids.

ACTIVITY

1. Place several items on a tray, and have the children determine whether the items are liquids or solids. Discuss the beginning letter of the name of each item.

2. As you examine each item, record the responses on the board or on a chart under columns labeled *Liquids* and *Solids*.

Liquids	Solids

3. You can extend this activity by taking photos of the items or having the children flip through magazines to find photos of liquids and solids. Print the item name under each photo, and place tape on the back of each.
4. As you determine whether an item is liquid or solid, ask a child to come up and place the photo in the appropriate column.

MINDING THE MATH

Encourage the children to count the number of items in each column and then graph the results. As an extension for older children, ask them to create math problems showing how many more or fewer items are in the columns as well as the total number of items in all.

LIQUIDS AND SOLIDS GRAPH

Number of Items		Solid	Liquid
6			
5			
4			
3			
2			
1			
		Solid	Liquid

Type of Item

LIQUID OR SOLID?

To deepen the children's understanding of solids and liquids, discuss that matter can change from one state to another. Review the properties of liquids and solids. Assist the children in filling ice-cube trays with water, and then put the trays in the freezer. The next day, show the children that the water has turned into a solid. Leave the trays out. When the ice cubes have melted, discuss that the water has returned to a liquid state.

The Mystery of Suspensions

CONCEPTS

The children will learn that suspensions have qualities of both liquids and solids and appear to be in a state between the two. Suspensions are thick; pour slowly; are similar to solids that appear to ooze; and can be compared to substances such as oobleck, GAK, or Silly Putty. The children will compare and contrast, mix, and measure as they explore a suspension.

DISCUSSION

Review with the children the properties of liquids and solids. Remind them that liquids, such as water, juice, and milk, pour. Demonstrate by pouring different liquids from one cup to another. (If you use a beverage other than water, pour it into cups for the children to drink so that the beverage is not wasted.) Then, note that you cannot pour solids. Demonstrate this by tapping a plastic lid or rock on the table.

Explain that today they will investigate another substance called a suspension. Suspensions appear to be both liquids and solids at times. How can this be? Suspensions are characterized by an in-between state. Explain to the children that they are going to make a suspension and then explore how it feels.

> **Note:** Although many children love putting their hands in gooey things, some children—including some with sensory issues—might not want to put their hands into the substance. It is okay if a child prefers to watch his friends touch the gooey stuff.

MATERIALS

For each group of four children:
- Tray
- Empty bowl or cup
- ½ cup cornstarch
- ¼ cup water (colored or plain)
- Plastic spoon

- Food coloring (optional)
- 2 cups
- Liquid, such as water, milk, or juice*
- Solid item, such as a rock or plastic lid
- Ziplock bags or plastic containers

*If you are using milk or juice for your demonstration, provide enough cups for each child to have some milk or juice to drink.

ACTIVITY

1. Go over the names of the materials on the tray. Write the names on the board and do not miss the opportunity to examine the first letter of each item.

2. Divide the children into groups of four. Tell them that everyone will have a chance to pour their ingredients into bowls to make a substance called *oobleck*.

3. Put a mixing bowl or cup in front of one child. Have him pour ¼ cup of colored water into the bowl. Pass the bowl to the next child, and have her pour in ½ cup of cornstarch. Pass the bowl to the next child, and ask her to stir the mixture. Let a fourth child pour it slowly out of the bowl and onto the table.

4. Invite the children to experiment with poking the mass on the table. When it is on the table or in the bowl, it appears to be a solid. The same will be true if the child holds it tightly in his hands. The pressure from the children's hands keeps the mass feeling like a solid. Once they open their hands, the oobleck will begin to ooze, forming a liquid-like state. As it oozes out of their hands and hits the table again, it will harden to a more solid state.

5. Let the groups of four children make batches of the oobleck from the materials on their trays. Encourage them to pour the substance onto the table.

6. Let them poke it, and discuss that it pours, but not quickly like water. As you poke it, discuss that it is like a solid as well. Give them a chance to freely explore the substance on the table.

7. When the children are finished exploring the oobleck, put the suspension mixtures in plastic containers or ziplock bags. When the children prepare to play with it in the future, have them wash or sanitize their hands first to keep germs away.

MINDING THE MATH

Using measuring cups is a great way to begin to talk about fractions. Show the children the markings on the cup, and talk with them about what the numbers mean.

Find the Long-Lost Animals

CONCEPTS

The children will learn about the role of a paleontologist, a scientist who studies fossils—the ancient remains of animals and plants. They will act as pretend paleontologists as they explore fossils with different plastic animals. The children will also sort by attributes and learn about characteristics of different types of dinosaurs. The follow-up activity provides opportunities to practice counting and learn the term *in half*.

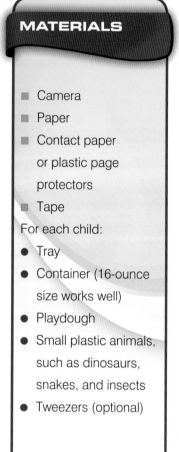

MATERIALS

- Camera
- Paper
- Contact paper or plastic page protectors
- Tape

For each child:

- Tray
- Container (16-ounce size works well)
- Playdough
- Small plastic animals, such as dinosaurs, snakes, and insects
- Tweezers (optional)

DISCUSSION

A doctor is a type of scientist. There are many types of doctors. Some check our teeth; they are called dentists. Others check our eyes (optometrists), and some doctors even check our feet (podiatrists). There are many other types of scientists. A paleontologist is a scientist who studies fossils. Fossils are remains of animals and plants, left behind when living things die. Some fossils are the bones of animals that are extinct or no longer around, such as dinosaurs. The children are going to pretend to be paleontologists and search for pretend fossils.

ACTIVITY

1. Take digital photos of the toy dinosaurs, snakes, and insects. Make charts with the specimen photos, and cover the chart with clear contact paper or place it in a plastic page protector. Tape it to the underside of each tray to use for sorting at the end of the activity.
2. Before working with the children, fill containers with playdough. Press the plastic animals inside each container.

3. Give each child a tray with pretend fossils. Have the children dump the contents of the containers onto their trays. Demonstrate how to pull the playdough apart and search for plastic dinos and other hidden critters. You can also give the children plastic tweezers to pick out their findings. Using tweezers as well as squeezing and ripping the playdough apart will also help the children with fine-motor skills.

4. Once the children have extracted all of the hidden treasures, instruct them to line up their specimens. Give each child a chance to point to each item and count how many he has found. This is a great way to practice one-to-one correspondence.

5. After the plastic toys have been extracted and counted, instruct the children to flip over their trays to reveal the charts of photos of the fossils. Have the children match up their items to the items in the photos. You can also discuss the names of the dinosaurs and other items as they are printed alongside the photos. Younger children can identify the first letter of each.

MINDING THE MATH

Encourage the children to sort the fossils by attributes such as insects versus dinosaurs, reptiles, and other animals. You can create a class graph and have the children contribute the number of fossils they found. Discuss the class findings. Afterward, the children can also use the graph to predict how many of each item they will find and then compare their findings.

At the end of the activity, have the children flatten the playdough into a pancake, which I call a "dinosaur burrito." Then instruct them to push the items back in, folding the burrito over before returning it to the plastic container. You can also introduce the term in half and ask the children to put their specimens on one half of the playdough before folding the other half on top.

After the activity, put the dinosaur burritos in your science center. Children love taking the playdough apart over and over again. Keep the exploration fresh by changing the items inside. Remind the children that they must wash or sanitize their hands before digging for fossils each time, to keep the playdough and hidden items clean.

Dealing with Density and Matter

CONCEPTS

The children will learn that some liquids are denser (heavier) than others. They will combine liquids and observe which float on top of the others. They will examine the words *sinking, floating, heavier,* and *lighter.* Children will predict; pour; analyze; use the positional words *top, middle,* and *bottom;* and discuss colors.

DISCUSSION

Mass, volume, and density are all properties of matter. In easy terms, mass is how much something weighs. Volume is how much space something takes up. Density is how much of matter is packed into a given space. A liquid that is very dense will seem to be heavier and will sink to the bottom of a cup, and something that is less dense will float to the top. Demonstrate how items sink or float by dropping them in your demonstration cup of water.

Then, discuss that everything is made of matter. Go around the room and name things; blocks, paper, crayons, toys, and even the children are matter. All matter has weight and takes up space. You can demonstrate this by picking up a block. Discuss that it takes up space, and if you drop it, its weight will cause it to fall.

Liquids are also matter. Show your demonstration cup, and discuss that the water takes up space in the cup. Pass around an empty cup and then the one with water so the children can feel the difference in weight.

Show the cups with the three different-colored liquids, and ask the children to tell you the colors. Discuss that the liquids each have a different amount of matter packed

MATERIALS

- Cup
- Water
- Variety of items to demonstrate sinking and floating
- Blue food coloring
- Red food coloring
- 2-liter bottle

For each child:
- Tray
- Paper towel
- 8-ounce clear plastic cup
- 2 ounces vegetable oil
- 2 ounces water colored blue
- 2 ounces corn syrup colored red

inside them. One of them will be very dense because it has more matter packed into the space than the other ones do. The dense liquid will sink to the bottom when the three liquids are combined; the less-dense liquids will float to the top.

ACTIVITY

1. Ahead of time, mix the blue food coloring into the water. Mix the red food coloring into the corn syrup. Pour a small amount of each of the three liquids—blue water, vegetable oil, and red corn syrup—into separate small cups.
2. On each child's tray, put down a paper towel and an empty 8-ounce plastic cup. Set up three 2-ounce drinking cups (or portion cups)—one with blue water, one with plain vegetable oil, and one with red corn syrup.
3. Instruct the children to pick up the cup with the yellow liquid—the oil—first and pour it into their clear, empty cup.
4. Have them pour the blue water into the cup with the oil. Like magic, the blue water will sink underneath the oil.
5. Remind the children of the concepts of sinking and floating, and ask them if the water is floating on the top or sinking to the bottom. The children should respond that the water sank to the bottom. The water sank because it is denser than the oil. The oil is lighter or less dense; therefore, it floats on top of the water.

6. Instruct the children to pour the red corn syrup into the cup with the oil and the water. They will be amazed to see the red corn syrup sink below the water.

7. Discuss what happened using the words *sink* and *float*. Discuss that the corn syrup is denser or heavier, so it sank to the bottom. Have the children look at their clear cup and ask them which liquid is on top, which is on the bottom, and which is in the middle.

8. You can pour all of the children's cups into one 2-liter bottle or large water bottle. Once the lid is on tight, you can turn the bottle and watch as the liquids combine, then separate again.

9. Try this activity using other liquids, and discuss the results.

LITERACY EXTENSION

Have the children draw their cups and label the colors red, yellow, and blue on their drawings.

The Estimation Guessing Game

CONCEPTS

Estimation is an important math skill. As children develop number sense, they will also develop their ability to estimate. Even young children can make predictions—the fun is in the guessing! Along with estimation, the children will sort items by size and will count the items in each category.

MATERIALS

- 3 clear bowls or containers
- 30–40 rubber balls of various sizes
- Slips of paper or sticky notes
- Crayons or pencils
- Whiteboard or chart paper
- Marker
- Paper-towel tubes
- Duct or masking tape

DISCUSSION

Write the word estimate on the board or on a piece of chart paper. Explain that when we make an *estimate,* we are making a guess. Even at a young age, children want to get things right, so explain that it does not matter if their guess is correct. Part of the fun is playing the guessing game.

ACTIVITY

1. Ahead of time, create a paper-towel ball holder by taping empty paper-towel tubes together with duct or masking tape. Set the ball holder aside.
2. Fill a container with rubber balls. Show the children the container. Take ten balls out of the container, and line them up on the table.
3. As you touch each ball, ask the children to help you count the balls. After the balls are counted, place them in an empty container.
4. Pass around the container so that the children can see how much space in the container is filled with the ten balls.
5. Show the children the balls that are left in the original container. Set the two containers side by side. Have the children look again at how much space is taken up by the ten balls, and have them estimate how many

balls are in the larger container. Let each child write her estimation on a slip of paper or sticky note. Help the younger children as needed.

6. Ask them to share their predictions. With older children, consider placing the sticky notes in numerical order on the board, creating a number line of sorts. Duplicate numbers can be put on top of each other.

7. Lay out the paper-towel ball holder, and give each child a handful of balls from the large container. Let them place the balls across the ball holder. When they have placed all the balls, it is time to start counting. Start at one end. As you touch each ball, model counting so that the children can join in. After the balls have been counted, compare the number of actual balls to the children's estimations.

MINDING THE MATH

Let the children sort the balls by size into three containers labeled *small, medium,* and *large.* Ask them to estimate how many balls they have in each category. Then, count each category with the children. Record your findings on a chart or graph.

REPORTING BALLS COUNTED

Small	Medium	Large

RUBBER-BALL GRAPH

Number of Balls			
20			
19			
18			
17			
16			
15			
14			
13			
12			
11			
10			
9			
8			
7			
6			
5			
4			
3			
2			
1			
	Small	Medium	Large
		Size of Balls	

Counting with Snapping Cubes or Teddy Bears

CONCEPTS

Give the children practice with estimating and counting. This activity works well after the Estimation Guessing Game to reinforce their learning.

DISCUSSION

When we make a prediction or estimation, we are guessing how many of a certain item will be in a container. Remember, it is okay if an estimation is not correct. After all, it is just a guess!

ACTIVITY

1. Give each pair or group of children a small bowl filled with snapping cubes or teddy-bear counters. In this activity, it is helpful if each bowl has the same amount of the item to be estimated. You can use more items in the bowl for older children. Snapping cubes work well because they snap together for easy counting.
2. Have the children estimate the number of cubes or teddy-bear counters in their bowl. They can write their estimations on sticky notes or slips of paper. Help younger children as needed.
3. Once the children have made their estimations, instruct them to dump out the cubes and snap them together. If using teddy-bear counters, they can simply line them up.
4. Assist the groups in counting the number of cubes from their bowls. Model touching each cube as you count it.
5. Ask the children to report their results. They can use a template like the one shown on the next page.

MATERIALS

For every group of two or three children:
- Bowl
- 25 snapping cubes or teddy-bear counters
- Sticky note or small slip of paper
- Pencil or crayon

REPORTING ON ESTIMATION AND COUNTING

Today I estimated snapping cubes in the science lab.

My estimate was _____ cubes.

I counted _____ cubes in all.

Hands-On Science and Math

The Weekly Estimation Jar

CONCEPTS

Estimating and making predictions are valuable skills that foster critical thinking in young children. The more children have opportunities to practice estimating, the better their estimating skills will become. This activity provides ideas for making estimation part of your daily routine.

MATERIALS

- Clear, plastic jar
- Sticky notes
- Pencils or markers
- Variety of items for estimating, such as rubber balls, marbles, plastic dinosaurs, and blocks

DISCUSSION

Use the same jar for estimating different items on different days. Introduce the children to the items in the jar for each lesson. Ask each child to estimate the number of items in the jar. You can also let them come up and write their estimations on the board or on a sticky note. If you use sticky notes, you can place the notes on the board and put them in numerical order. If more than one child has the same estimation, those notes can be placed together in a column to form a sort of graph.

ACTIVITY

1. Set up an estimation jar in your classroom to use on a regular basis. Be sure to keep the container the same, but vary the items in the jar.
2. On one day of the week, bring the jar into your circle time or math time, and have the children look at the jar and develop their predictions.
3. The next day, allow time for estimation to take place by asking each child to write an estimate either on a sticky note or on the board.

4. On the third day, dump out the items, and count them together. The more you make this a part of your routine, the better the children will become at estimating close to the actual number and understanding spatial relationships.

MINDING THE MATH

Make an estimation booklet or log for each child. As they become better at the skill of estimation, have them write or copy the name of the item to be estimated as well as their estimation and the results. For younger children, you can write the item name for them, and then you can help them write the numbers.

Item name: _____

My estimate: _____

Number of items in the estimation jar: _____

Building Strong Structures

CONCEPTS

In this activity, children will learn how columns are used to increase the strength of a building. They will be amazed to find how much weight six ordinary sheets of paper can hold. The children will practice counting as they determine the number of books the paper structure can hold.

MATERIALS

- 12 sheets of copy paper
- Tape
- Stack of similarly sized books

DISCUSSION

Explain that buildings need to be constructed on strong foundations so that they are safe for the people inside. Tell the children that they are going to build a structure using paper and tape that will support the weight of several books. Ask the children if they think that a piece of paper is strong. Explain that when the paper is rolled to make a round column, it becomes very strong.

ACTIVITY

1. Roll up a sheet of paper loosely, so that the opening is about an inch in diameter. Create a column 8½ inches high, and tape it in three places. Repeat for five more sheets.
2. Roll up each of the other six pieces of paper tightly into 8½-inch columns, and tape them.
3. Begin using the bigger columns and place them as shown in the diagram. Use a book that you will be stacking on top of the columns as your guide. Place the four outer columns underneath the corners of your book; place the two remaining columns in the center.

4. Ask the children to predict whether the narrow or wide columns will hold the most weight. Most children will predict the bigger ones, but in truth, the smaller ones rolled tightly will actually hold more weight.

5. Have the children guess how many books they think can be stacked on top of the bigger paper columns. Write the predictions on the board so you can compare the results in the end.

6. Carefully stack one book on top of the six columns. The structure may be a bit wobbly, but it will become steadier once the second book is added. After placing the second book on top, have each child, one at a time, bring you another book to be stacked.

7. As you continue stacking, count how many books are being supported. Be sure the children are not too close to the structure, so no one gets hurt when it comes crashing down.

8. After the columns break, count again the total number of books that were supported by the big columns.

9. Repeat the activity using the columns that are wound more tightly. They will hold more books. Review the findings, and compare them to the children's predictions.

MINDING THE MATH

Repeat this activity for more practice with counting. You can use heavier or lighter books, and you can change the placement of the columns. Older children can use a scale to weigh the books and figure out how much weight was supported by the structure.

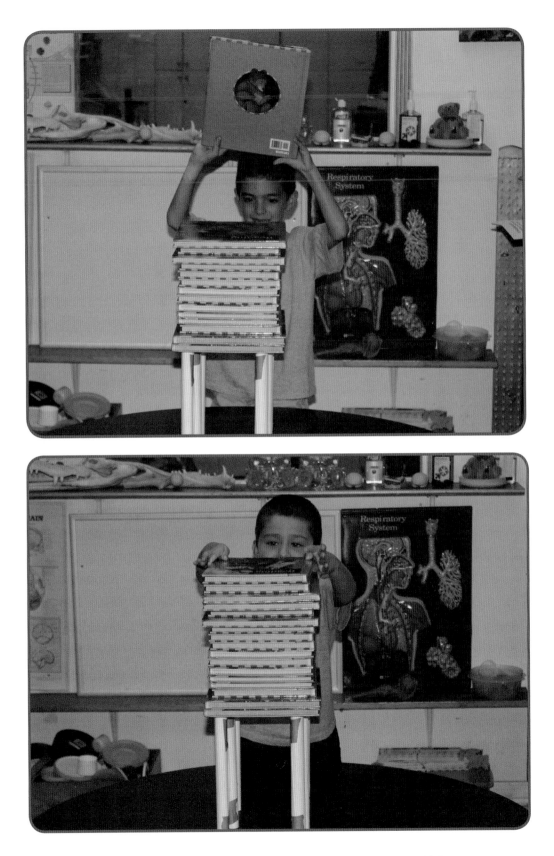

Changing, Bubbling, and Rolling

Children are fascinated when they recognize how substances can change and combine to alter their properties. Experimenting with blending colors can help children see physical changes as they occur. Similarly, making mixtures helps children understand chemical changes. When they observe a transformation from one color to another, from one texture to another, or from a static state to a bubbling movement, for example, they can use their own senses to appreciate how science works in their world. These types of lessons are so much more effective when children see the wonder of change with their own eyes, feel it with their own hands, and begin to understand it with their hungry minds.

Let the Color Changes Flow!

CONCEPTS

The children will make predictions about the hues different primary colors can make. Children will learn about change as they explore how to combine primary colors to make secondary hues.

MATERIALS

- Variety of items in primary colors
- Food coloring or liquid watercolor

For each pair of children:

- 2 pipettes
- Small container of red water
- Small container of yellow water
- Small container of blue water
- Cup of plain water
- Plastic flower tray with multiple sections or foam egg carton

DISCUSSION

Have various items of different colors on display. Review the primary colors of red, yellow, and blue. Tell the children that when they mix these colors, they can create new colors called secondary colors. Challenge them to predict what secondary colors will be made with different combinations of primary colors.

ACTIVITY

1. Pair the children, so that they can share water and use their own pipettes to mix colors.
2. Prior to this activity, the children should have learned how to use a pipette to draw up water. Demonstrate and review the proper use, and give them opportunities to practice drawing up clean water into their pipettes.
3. Explain that they will, on your direction, combine two colors to make a new color.
4. Direct the children to fill their pipettes with red and to put the liquid in an empty space in the flower tray or egg carton.
5. Emphasize the importance of cleaning the droppers by drawing up rinse water and squirting it out before placing their pipettes in the next color.

6. Have the children add a pipette of yellow to the red. Ask them to notice what new color is created.

7. Repeat the process using red and blue.

8. Repeat the process using blue and yellow.

MINDING THE MATH

As the children drip colored water from their pipettes, count the number of drops out loud with them. How many drops do their droppers hold?

Squish and Squeeze: Secondary Colors

CONCEPTS

The children will blend primary colored paint in bags to create secondary colors. They will use their hands to do the blending, which will give them a chance to learn the lesson via a sensory experience.

MATERIALS

- Plastic spoons
- White fingerpaint paper (optional)

For each child or pair:

- Ziplock bag
- 2 primary colors of tempera or fingerpaint

DISCUSSION

Review how two primary colors can blend to form a secondary color. Ask what new color is made when red and yellow are combined. How about red and blue or yellow and blue? Tell the children that they will combine primary colors in bags and use their hands to mix the colors and make new ones.

ACTIVITY

1. Place a spoonful of each of two different primary colors of tempera paint in a ziplock bag. Make enough bags for each child or pair of children.
2. Seal the bags, and have the children squish and squeeze the colors in the bags until the hues change to secondary colors.
3. The children can draw with their fingers through the bags to press the paint away and make designs.
4. If you like, the children can tape or hang the bags in the window so the light shines through. The bags can form decorations for the classroom.
5. You can also open the bags and let the children use the paint to fingerpaint pictures.

MINDING THE MATH

Seal the bags, and tape the seams. Place the colorful bags in your math manipulatives area for children to practice writing numbers with their fingers through the bags.

LITERACY EXTENSION

Use the bags for a writing extension. Place the colorful bags in your writing area for the children to practice writing letters with their fingers through the bags.

Absorbing Color Combinations

CONCEPTS

The children will examine the concept of absorption using colored water to make the process more visible. Afterward, they will review their results and graph the outcome.

MATERIALS

- Small cup
- Paper towels, cut in strips lengthwise
- Water
- Red, yellow, and blue food coloring

For each pair of children:

- 3 small containers
- 1 strip of paper towel, cut lengthwise
- 2 primary colors of water
- Stopwatch (optional)

DISCUSSION

Begin by telling the children they are going to see a magic trick. Pour a small amount of water on the table, and explain that the paper towel you are holding is magical. Drop the paper towel on the spot of water, and tell the children to say abracadabra as you wipe up the water. Pick up the paper towel, and explain that it made the water disappear.

Afterward, explain that it was not really magic; the paper towel absorbed the water from the table. Have the children repeat the word *absorb,* and explain that when something absorbs, it picks up liquids. Discuss other things that absorb, such as bath towels, sponges, and so on. Let them know that they will have a chance to experiment with absorbing colors.

ACTIVITY

1. Demonstrate the absorption activity by placing containers of yellow and blue water on the table with an empty container in the middle. Place one end of the folded paper towel in the container of yellow water and the other end in the container of blue water. Push the towel ends into the bottom of the containers. Be sure the middle of the paper towel is resting on the empty container.

2. Ask the children to watch and observe as the blue and yellow water absorb up the paper towel. When the colors meet, they will combine to form green.

3. To continue the activity and let them learn by doing, give each pair of children a similar setup. Vary the primary colors you give each pair so that they will create various secondary colors.

4. Have the children put the ends of their paper towels into different containers of colored water. Let them watch as the paper absorbs the water and the colors move toward the middle of the towel, which is resting on the empty container. When the two primary colors absorb into the middle, a new secondary color will form.

5. Incorporate math by having the children count how long it takes for the water to get to the center of the paper towel strip and combine to make the new color. Older children can record this data and graph the time it took for each strip to fully absorb the water.

6. The children will want to do this absorption activity again and again. If time allows, continue handing out additional strips, and have the children place them in the colored water one on top of the other. The more strips they use, the faster the water will absorb and meet in the middle. They can continue tracking the time for each strip.

7. When all groups are done, review the various combinations of primary colors the children started with and the secondary colors they produced.
   - Blue and yellow produced green.
   - Blue and red produced purple.
   - Red and yellow produced orange.

MINDING THE MATH

Older children can count or use a stopwatch to measure how long it takes for the two colors of water to absorb and combine to produce a secondary color. Younger children can count how many primary and secondary colors the class used. The children can also count and graph how many of each new color they produced. Graphing options include drawing the graph on the board and having the children place an X in the box or color it in, using snapping cubes to create a three-dimensional graph, or posting sticky notes in columns on the board. The class could also use a pocket chart.

HOW MANY COLORS?

How Many	Orange	Purple	Green
9			
8			
7			
6			
5			
4			
3			
2			
1			

Secondary Colors

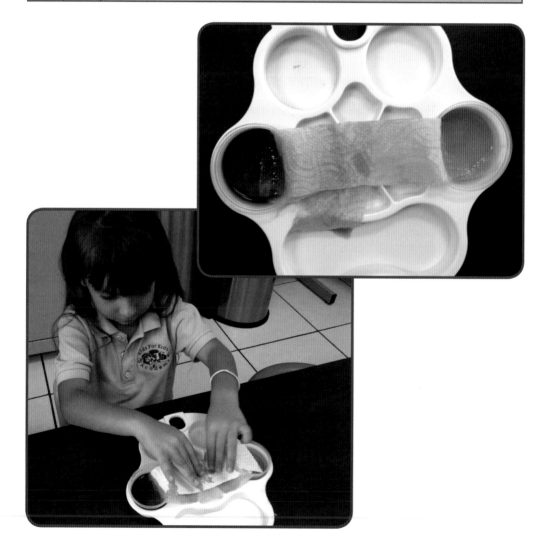

Fluffed-Up Soap

CONCEPTS

The children will learn about the physical properties of matter and the terms *hot, cold, sinking,* and *floating.* They will observe physical changes in a bar of soap after it is heated in the microwave and will have opportunities to touch, smell, and explore the soap in its new form.

DISCUSSION

Begin by reviewing the concept that anything that has weight and takes up space is matter. A block is matter. If you drop it, it will fall to the ground because it has weight. It also takes up space on the table. Continue mentioning random items around the room and pointing out that they are all matter. All matter has physical properties, such as the item's size, shape, or color. If you change the physical properties of matter, you are still left with the original matter.

To demonstrate this idea, hold up a piece of paper, and ask the children what you are holding. Crumple it. Ask if it is still paper. Then, flatten it out and color on it. Ask if it is still paper. Rip it in half. Ask if it is still paper. Explain that it is still paper because only the physical properties have changed. In this experiment, you will change the physical properties of a bar of soap, yet the end product will still be soap.

MATERIALS

- Shoe box–size, rectangular, microwave-safe container
- 1 bar of Ivory soap (This brand has the properties needed.)
- Container of water
- Bowl for each child
- Microwave
- Whiteboard or chart paper
- Marker

ACTIVITY

1. Take a bar of Ivory soap out of its wrapper. Ask the children, "What is this?" Pass it around so that the children can use their senses to feel and smell the soap. Ask, "What color is the bar of soap?" "What is its shape?" Bang it on the table, and ask if it is a solid or liquid.

2. Ask the children if they think the bar of soap will sink or float when placed in water. Count the number of predictions, then record them on the board or a tablet.

3. Ask the children to observe what happens when you drop the bar of soap into the container of water. You will find that the bar of soap floats. This is not true with all bars, but it is the case with Ivory.

4. Ask the children if they know what a microwave does to items inside it when the oven is turned on. Many will say that it cooks or makes things hot. Ask the children to predict what they think will happen when a bar of soap is placed in a microwave. Some might say that it will get hot; others will predict that it will melt. After the children have a chance to share, write their predictions on the board or chart.

5. Place the wet bar of soap in the shoe box–size container, and put it in the microwave. Set the timer for 2 minutes 30 seconds.

6. Everyone will be amazed when the microwave door opens. The once-small, rectangular bar of soap will have filled the box with a huge mass of white fluff.

7. Show the children how fluffy it is by touching the top—but only the top—with your hands.

> **CAUTION:** Do not press down on the fluff until it cools because the interior will be very hot. Do not let the children touch the fluffy soap until it has cooled for about 30 seconds. Use that time to discuss the physical properties of the soap fluff that the children can see.

8. When the fluff has cooled enough to be safe, rip off pieces, and hand a piece to each child.

9. Allow them to squeeze the fluff and rub it between their hands. If you ask them to do this over a bowl or paper towel, they can turn their piece of fluff into powder.

> **CAUTION:** The soap powder may make some children sneeze from the strong scent.

10. Collect all of the powder into a bowl, and ask if it is still soap. The answer is yes because only the physical properties have changed. If the smell does not bother the

children, you can put the container of soap powder in a sensory bin in your discovery area.

11. You may find that a hot piece of soap is left on the bottom of the container. If you like, you can place it back in the microwave for one minute, and you will have another piece of soap fluff. Again, be careful of the heat inside the fluff!

12. The children will have fun when they go to the sink to wash their hands after the activity because they will not need to apply soap.

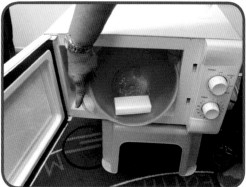

MINDING THE MATH

As the microwave counts down, point out the numbers on the timer and how they are counting backward. For older children, discuss that there are 60 seconds in a minute. As the microwave reaches 60 seconds, model counting backward until the timer goes off.

Chemical Changes: Making a Mixture

CONCEPTS

The children will combine ingredients to create a chemical change. The original ingredients will no longer be able to be separated—they will have become a new substance: playdough! They will also measure, mix, and use their motor skills to knead and fold.

MATERIALS

For the demonstration:
- Box of muffin or cake mix
- Egg
- Flour
- Sugar
- Salt
- Yeast
- Milk
- 5 small ziplock bags
- Measuring cup for each child
- Large mixing bowl
- Large ziplock bag or airtight container
- Whiteboard or chart paper
- Marker

Recipe for one batch of playdough:
- 3 cups flour
- 1½ cups salt
- 1 cup water
- ¼ cup vegetable oil
- Food coloring

(Multiply the playdough recipe if needed to make enough for all the children to play with a portion at the end of the activity.)

DISCUSSION

Before beginning the discussion, open the muffin- or cake-mix box, take the bag of mix out, and set it aside. Fill the box with small bags of ingredients such as flour, sugar, salt, milk, and yeast. Put an egg into the box as well. Note: Consider having baked goods on hand for the children to eat after the lesson. Because you are working with food, that could emphasize some children's insecure food situations.

Explain that when a chemical change takes place, we cannot get the original ingredients back, and a new product is produced. In the Fluffed-Up Soap activity, we discussed that if you color, fold, or rip a piece of paper, it is still paper. All you have done is change its physical properties. However, if you had burned the paper, then it would have turned to ash, which would have been a chemical change rather than a physical change.

Tell the children that the class is going to combine ingredients to make something new. Explain that once we mix everything together, we will not be able to get the individual items back. When starting the lesson, take each item out of the muffin- or cake-mix box, and talk about how all these ingredients make up the cake or muffins that you eat. Explain that once you put the ingredients together and bake them, you cannot take them apart again. Making playdough, cake, or muffins provides an example of a chemical change. Introduce the children to the playdough recipe and the separate ingredients that will go into the mixture. Write the recipe on a large piece of paper or on the board.

ACTIVITY

1. Divide the playdough ingredients into small quantities to allow all of the children to participate. If you have twelve children, for example, you could double the recipe and have twelve containers of ingredients for the children to hold and pour. Let the children help you measure the ingredients into their measuring cups.
2. Pass around the large bowl, and have each child pour in an ingredient. Add the flour first, then the water, and follow with the other ingredients.
3. After all the children have poured in their ingredients, fold in the ingredients and keep folding until the mixture has a smooth consistency. Let the children dig in and help with the mixing. As you work, talk with the children about how the ingredients have changed. You cannot pull out the flour or the water or the food coloring. The ingredients have become something new.
4. When the consistency is just right, give each child a portion of playdough, and allow time for free exploration.

MINDING THE MATH

Measuring helps children connect a number with its meaning, a concept called numeracy. Let the children measure the ingredients for the playdough into their measuring cups. In combining the ingredients for the playdough, talk with the children about amounts and use vocabulary such as more and less.

LITERACY EXTENSION

Invite the children to roll their playdough into snakes and use the playdough snakes to form the letters of their names. The rolling and pinching of the snakes as they make letters is also great for fine-motor development.

Bubbling Baking Soda

CONCEPTS

You will demonstrate how two substances can be mixed to produce a gas. The children will use their senses of sight, hearing, and smell.

DISCUSSION

If you have completed the Chemical Changes lesson, remind the children that when you combine the ingredients of flour, water, salt, oil, and food coloring, you produce new matter—playdough. A chemical change takes place, and you are unable to get the original ingredients back. In this activity, they will combine vinegar and baking soda to produce something new, a gas. You will not be able to see the gas because it is invisible, but you will be able to see evidence of the change by watching a balloon. Even though we cannot see a gas, it takes up space.

ACTIVITY

1. Explain that vinegar at the bottom of a test tube will be mixed with baking soda inside a balloon. Have the children predict what will happen.
2. For demonstration purposes, place 2 ounces of vinegar at the bottom of the test tube (or water bottle). Use a funnel to put 1 tablespoon of baking soda into the balloon.
3. Carefully stretch the opening of the balloon over the mouth of the test tube, and hold it tight at that spot with one hand. With your other hand, hold up the other end of the balloon, and shake the baking soda into the test tube.

MATERIALS

For your demonstration:
- Test tube or 8-ounce water bottle
- Funnel
- 2 ounces vinegar
- 1 tablespoon baking soda
- Balloon
- Timer or stopwatch

For each child:
- Egg carton or recycled lids
- Pipette or dropper
- ¼ cup vinegar
- ½ teaspoon baking soda
- Red, yellow, and blue food coloring

4. Ask the children to observe what happens to the balloon. When the two ingredients are mixed, fizzing will take place at the bottom of the test tube, and the balloon will begin to inflate.

5. Note that you created a gas, which is causing the balloon to inflate. Emphasize that the gas is new matter that was produced by mixing the vinegar and baking soda together. Explain that, because you cannot get either ingredient back, a chemical change has taken place.

6. Move around the room, and let the children feel the balloon.

7. Following the demonstration, put about ½ teaspoon of baking soda in a section of each child's egg carton or in a lid. In separate sections, provide about a teaspoon of vinegar in each of the three colors—red, yellow, and blue—for each child.

8. Allow the children to fill their pipettes with colored vinegar and drop the vinegar onto the baking soda in their containers. Ask them to listen and watch as the baking soda fizzes inside the trays.

9. Let the children experiment with dropping different colors of vinegar on the same batches of baking soda. They will see that the combination not only fizzes, but it also changes colors. They find this visible change very exciting!

MINDING THE MATH

Using a timer or stopwatch (or the app on a smartphone), measure how long ½ teaspoon of baking soda and a few drops of vinegar will fizz. How long will ¼ teaspoon of baking soda and a drop of vinegar fizz? How long will a teaspoon of baking soda and a teaspoon of vinegar fizz? Ask the children to observe the differences, and talk with them about why they think this happens.

Look Out! Volcano Erupting

CONCEPTS

While creating a simulated volcano that erupts, the children will explore the concepts of chemical change, creating a gas, and how volcanic eruptions occur.

DISCUSSION

Use a computer or tablet device to show video clips of an erupting volcano. You can also bring in photos of real eruptions. Explain that when a volcano erupts, lava—rock so hot that it has melted—is forced out of the ground and spills out of the volcano. Explain that in this activity, they will make a pretend volcano.

MATERIALS

For each pair of children:

- Paper bowl
- 4-ounce paper cup
- Funnel
- 2 tablespoons baking soda
- 2 ounces vinegar
- Red food coloring

ACTIVITY

1. Use food coloring to turn the vinegar red, and give each pair of children a 2-ounce portion, along with the other materials and ingredients.
2. For each pair, place the paper cup into the small disposable bowl, and put the baking soda in the bottom of the cup. Alternatively, give the children portion cups holding the baking soda, and allow them to pour the baking soda into their drinking cups.
3. Tell the children to place their funnels inside their cups and quickly pour the vinegar into the top of the funnel.
4. Because the children get so excited watching the eruptions, have one pair of students at a time do their demonstration. The children will not get bored watching this over and over again!

On the board, draw the cup with the funnel and the red mixture pouring out of it. Label the cup and the funnel. Have the children draw their own depiction of the experiment, and assist them in writing a sentence about what happened.

Launching Recycled Rockets

CONCEPTS

Space and space travel are exciting topics for children. Most will know that rockets go up into outer space and that space is a faraway place. This activity involves recycling paper-towel tubes to make rockets. The children will be amazed when the rockets launch high in the air. Concepts presented include following directions, counting, making predictions, and understanding the concept of chemical changes in matter.

DISCUSSION

Outer space is far, far away, and to get there astronauts (space travelers) cannot get in their cars or take a plane. They travel to space in a rocket ship. In this activity, a chemical change will take place. When the antacid tablet and the water are combined, they release a gas, which will shoot the pretend rocket in the air.

ACTIVITY

1. You might want to do this activity outside to allow room for the rocket to blast off.
2. To create the rocket exterior, have each child tape a recycled plastic lid to the top of half a paper-towel tube.
3. Let the children take turns launching their own rockets. For each one, fill a plastic canister partway with water. If you use the M&M's container, fill it one-third full. If you use a film canister, fill it half full. You can also put the water in a test tube and let the child pour it into the canister.

MATERIALS

For each child:
- Safety glasses or goggles
- Half a paper-towel tube
- Small plastic canister with a lid that snaps inside (mini M&M's candies tubes work well if you cut the strip attached to the lid, and so do film canisters)
- Water
- Half of a calcium carbonate antacid tablet, such as Alka-Seltzer
- Plastic lid that extends over the cardboard tube
- Masking tape
- Test tube (optional)

4. Give each child half of an antacid tablet. Be sure their hands are dry; wet tablets will not work. With the child close to you, have him place the tablet into the water.
5. Then you—not the child—should quickly attach the lid, snapping it on tightly.
6. Turn the container over, and put the paper-towel tube on top. You and the child should move away and count how long it takes for the rocket to blast off. The liquid and antacid will spill out as the rocket blasts off.
7. Repeat so that each child has a chance to launch a rocket.
8. If you experiment with the amount of water, you will find that the less water, the higher the rocket will go. Just below half of the canister tends to work well.

MINDING THE MATH

When the children launch their rockets, leave the lids where they have landed (most will come off of the rocket). You can have each child count the number of footsteps from the launch pad to where her rocket landed. You can even graph the data.

LITERACY EXTENSION

Read books about the solar system or space travel. Have the children draw rockets blasting off. Write the words *rocket, clouds, sun,* and *sky* on the board. Tell the children to include these elements in their pictures. They can label their pictures using the words written on the board.

Go, Car, Go! Simple Machines and Inclined Planes

CONCEPTS

The children will learn about how simple machines make work easier. They will be introduced to the concepts of an inclined plane, potential energy, and kinetic energy. When they practice rolling cars down ramps, they will learn that the higher the ramp, the farther the car will roll. They will exercise the skills of counting and measurement, including nonstandard measurement.

DISCUSSION

When you think of machines, you probably think of cars, trucks, or power tools. All of these machines need motors to make them work. There are machines that do not need motors, such as bottle openers, scissors, screws, wheels, or hammers. An inclined plane is a simple machine that helps you do work without moving. Suppose you want to put your bicycle in the back of a truck. You can use a board wide enough for your bicycle and long enough to reach from the ground to the bed of the truck on a gradual slope. If you used a longer board to make the inclined plane, you would need less force or effort to move your bicycle, but you would have to move it a longer distance.

In this activity, you will find out if increasing the level of an inclined plane will make a toy car roll farther. When you place a car at the top of an inclined plane, there is potential energy (stored energy) in the car. When the car is released, the energy is converted to kinetic energy (energy in motion). The farther above ground the inclined plane is, the greater potential energy it has.

ACTIVITY

1. Tell the children that they will each have a role to play in this experiment. Draw a chart to record the data. For older children, let a volunteer be the recorder. For each step, choose a different child to assist in either letting go of the car, counting the steps to reach the rolled car, or adding books to the stack.
2. Place two books on the ground. Place one end of the toy car track on top of the books and one end on the floor.
3. Have a child place a car at the top of the track, making sure all four wheels are on the track. Tell him to release the car.
4. Measure how many "feet" the car traveled by having another child pace off the steps from the end of the ramp to where the car rolled. Ask the recorder to write down the number. You can also measure the distance with a yardstick or measuring tape.
5. Repeat the steps, adding two books to the pile each time.

MINDING THE MATH

Use these charts and graphs to record the data in this experiment.

TRACKING BOOKS AND DISTANCE

Number of Books	Distance Traveled in Steps
2	
4	
6	

CLASS GRAPH OF CAR-ROLLING RESULTS

Distance in Steps		2 Books	4 Books	6 Books
	18			
	16			
	14			
	12			
	10			
	8			
	6			
	4			
	2			
	0			

Number of Books on the Ramp

LITERACY EXTENSION

To summarize the results, write the three sentences below on the board. Have older children copy them onto their papers. With younger children, you can simply ask them to tell you the answers, and you can fill in the blanks on the board. Point out the number words *two, four,* and *six.* Help the children transfer the data from the graph into their sentences. Under the sentences, each child should draw a picture of the stack of books with the ramp and the car rolling off. Ask them to label their pictures with the words *books, car,* and *ramp.*

Use the data table or the graph to summarize your results.

When two books were used, the car traveled _____ steps.

When four books were used, the car traveled _____ steps.

When six books were used, the car traveled _____ steps.

4

Cooking, Looking, and Listening

Children interpret the world through their senses. As the children you are working with learn about temperature changes, being able to feel the difference between hot and cold makes the concepts real to them. Preparing hot and cold foods gives the children hands-on opportunities to explore temperature differences and the energy used to create those changes in food. If you incorporate cooking into your curriculum regularly, you will provide the children with opportunities to count, measure, and understand the importance of following directions. You can relate cooking activities to the weekly theme as a way to make abstract concepts more concrete. For example, a lesson on geometrical shapes might be followed up with the children making cookies of various shapes. Similarly, a lesson on color might tie in with an activity making chilled gelatin or pudding of that color. Just remember that any cooking activity should be safe. Also, if you are doing an activity involving food or food ingredients, the activity should allow the children to eat the food to avoid adding challenges for children whose food availability is insecure. Plus you will give them a taste of science and math that they will never forget!

Beyond cooking, as the children begin to understand temperature changes, they can explore different energy sources, such as light and sound, and the powerful effects they can have in their world.

It's Snowing Inside!

MATERIALS

- Test tube with lid or glass baby-food jar
- Water
- Calcium chloride, such as DampRid, found in the supermarket detergent aisle
- Instant snow, such as Insta-Snow, available from science or school-supply sites online
- Plastic container for each child
- Photos or clip art of hot things, such as pizza, coffee, the sun, children in bathing suits
- Photos or clip art of cold things, such as ice cream, ice, orange juice, snow, children in winter clothing
- Large plastic container
- Whiteboard or chart paper
- Marker
- Digital thermometer

CONCEPTS

The children will learn about temperature and the difference between hot and cold. They will participate in activities that let them feel how chemical reactions can make substances hot or cold. The children will explore the sounds of the letters *H* and *C* and also will distinguish between pictures of hot and cold items.

DISCUSSION

Temperature tells us the condition of the air outside. In some places, it is very hot, and in some places it is very cold. Tell the children that they are going to feel things that are hot and cold. Write the words *hot* and *cold* on the board or on a piece of paper. Ask what letter each word starts with and review the sounds of *H* and *C*. As you show the children a picture, ask if the item is hot or cold. When you hold up the photos of the clothing, ask if the clothing is worn when it is hot or cold outside. Encourage the children to make inferences regarding the clothing. Why are the children on the beach wearing shorts? The weather is hot. Why is the boy wearing mittens? Snow is cold.

ACTIVITY

1. Place a heaping tablespoon of calcium chloride in the test tube or baby-food jar, and add water. The baby-food jar works better because it has a metal lid, which will feel hot.

> **CAUTION:** The calcium chloride is toxic and should only be handled by the teacher.

2. Place the lid on, and shake the jar well. The jar or test tube will get hot. Pass the container around the group, and let the children feel what hot feels like.

3. Tell the children that you are going to make pretend snow in their hands. Have each child make a cup with her hands. Put one of your hands under the child's, and pour one scoop of instant snow into her hands. (I have found that Insta-Snow works best for this activity.) Then, pour cold water into the child's cupped hands to fill them up. Wait while the powder and water turn to a snowlike consistency right before her eyes!

4. Put an empty container under the child's hands so she can drop the snow and explore it with her fingers. I make extra snow and put it in the children's containers after they have made their own snow.

5. Once everyone has had the experience of feeling the instant snow, put it in a container for later use and exploration. If you put the instant snow in the freezer, it will stay cold. If it starts to dehydrate, just add more water. Be sure that the children wash their hands before handling the snow to keep it clean.

MINDING THE MATH

Using a digital thermometer, find the temperature of the water with the calcium chloride. Compare it to the temperature of the cold water or the snow. Discuss which number is greater.

LITERACY EXTENSION

Have the children smooth out the snow in their containers. Call out letters and encourage them to use their fingers to make the letters in the snow. Spell out the words *hot* and *cold,* and have the children write those words in their containers of snow.

Shake and Freeze:
Homemade Ice Cream

CONCEPTS

Cooking activities provide a way to demonstrate hot and cold. By involving the children in making ice cream, you can reinforce the concept of chemical change as you make a yummy treat.

DISCUSSION

Ice cream is always a popular treat. To make it, we combine different ingredients. When the ingredients freeze together, a chemical change takes place, and we have something new—ice cream. The process involves a chemical change because once the mixture turns into ice cream, we cannot get the individual ingredients out. In this activity, we can freeze the ice cream without even using a freezer! When salt is added to ice, it actually makes the temperature of the ice even colder, which makes it possible to freeze the ingredients into ice cream.

ACTIVITY

1. Divide the children into groups of four. Give each group a set of materials. Ask the groups to watch as you demonstrate how to do the activity.
2. Fill a gallon-size plastic bag about half full with ice cubes, and put the salt in the bag.
3. Call up children one at a time to assist in putting the milk, vanilla, and sugar in a quart-size ziplock bag.
4. Squeeze out the air, and seal the smaller bag.
5. Put the quart-size bag filled with ingredients into the large bag of ice and salt. Squeeze out as much air as possible, and seal the large bag. It is important that you seal the bag completely. If you like, you can

MATERIALS

- Plastic spoons
- Bowls or cups
- Timer or stopwatch

For your demonstration and for each group of four children:

- Gallon-size, heavy-duty ziplock bag or large coffee can with lid
- Sandwich- or quart-size ziplock bag or small coffee can with lid
- Ice
- 6 tablespoons salt
- ½ cup milk
- 1 tablespoon sugar
- ¼ teaspoon vanilla extract
- Duct tape

substitute two metal coffee cans—large and small—for the bags. The inside can should have the ice-cream ingredients. Be sure to tape the can closed with duct tape. Place the smaller can inside the larger can, which will contain the ice and salt.

6. Have two children each hold a corner of the bag and shake it back and forth until the mixture inside gets thick. The bag will get very cold, so have the children take turns. The faster the bag is shaken back and forth, the less time the process will take. You may want to hold the bag at each end and shake rapidly for three minutes before giving the children a chance. Because the bag gets very cold, the children may not be able to shake it for the entire time needed, which is about five minutes. If using coffee cans, the children can roll the outer can back and forth to mix the ingredients inside the smaller can.

7. Remove the small bag of ice cream, and wipe the salt off the bag.

8. Let the children do the activity for themselves, then everyone can enjoy a frosty treat!

MINDING THE MATH

To reinforce the process of turning a liquid to a frozen state, place an unfrozen, liquid freezer pop in a gallon-size ziplock bag. Fill the bag with ice and ½ cup of salt. Seal the bag completely, and have the children take turns shaking the bag. Use a timer or stopwatch to time how long it takes for the ice pop to freeze. Be sure to shake continuously until the ice pop is frozen, which should take about six minutes.

Sun-Cooked Snacks

CONCEPTS

A perfect sunny-day activity, the children will learn about the role the sun plays in producing heat. They will also use the power of the sun to actually cook fun s'mores treats. Finally, children will learn about the dangers of the sun and ways to protect themselves from its powerful rays.

MATERIALS

- Large cardboard box, such as a copy-paper box
- Black tempera paint
- Aluminum foil
- Clear plastic lid or sheet of acrylic plastic
- Thermometer

For each child:

- 2 small butter cookies or graham-cracker segments
- ½ large marshmallow
- 1 rectangle of a chocolate bar
- 8" x 8" piece of aluminum foil or black paper plate
- Paintbrush
- Paint smock
- Paper cup

DISCUSSION

While discussing the word *hot,* talk about the energy that the sun produces, and note that we can use that energy for cooking. Tell the children that you are going to make a solar cooker and use it to cook s'mores. You will put a thermometer in the cooker and record the temperature. Explain to the children that you will paint the box black because black absorbs more light and gives off more heat than other colors. You can share that when you wear a black shirt in the summer, you feel hotter than when you wear a white shirt. White reflects the light, while black absorbs it and then emits the energy as heat. You will put aluminum foil inside the box to act like a mirror and reflect the light from the sun onto the food in the box. A clear plastic cover on top of the box will allow the light in and will help trap the heat inside.

ACTIVITY

1. Have the children assist in making the solar oven. Let them put on paint smocks to protect their clothes. Put some black tempera paint into paper cups, and give each child a paintbrush. The children can help paint

the outside of the large box black. Set the box aside to dry. Once the paint dries, line the inside of the box with aluminum foil.

2. Using the thermometer, measure the temperature inside the box. Show the children the starting temperature on the thermometer, and record the temperature. Lay the thermometer inside the box.

3. Give each child s'mores ingredients and a piece of aluminum foil or a black paper plate. Show them how to put the bottom cookie down first and then lay a marshmallow half on the cookie. Top each marshmallow with a rectangle of chocolate. Leave the top cookie off for now.

4. Set the box outside in the sun. Place the s'mores inside the box, and cover the box with the clear plastic cover or plastic wrap. This will trap the heat inside the box (and keep bugs out).

5. Watch to see when the chocolate melts. On a hot day, the cooking should take less than five minutes.

6. While the s'mores are in the solar oven, you can discuss how dangerous the sun can be. Remind the children of the importance of using sunscreen to protect themselves from the burning rays of the sun.

7. Carefully remove the foil pieces or plates, and hand them out to the children. Let the children put the other cookie pieces on top of their s'mores. Tell them to press gently to make the ooey-gooey marshmallows squish out a little. Enjoy!

MINDING THE MATH

When the s'mores are done, check the thermometer inside the solar oven. What temperature does it read? Talk with the children about the temperature inside the box before the activity, and compare it to the temperature after the activity. Which temperature is higher? Why did the temperature change?

Creative Printing with Sunlight

CONCEPTS

The sun is a powerful energy source. In this activity, the children will see the power of the sun firsthand as they create images fixed onto paper by sunlight. Reserve this activity for a sunny day for the best effect.

MATERIALS

- Sun-sensitive paper, such as Sunprint, or dark blue construction paper
- Various items to arrange on paper, such as nuts, bolts, keys, tiny plastic dinosaurs or insects, buttons, or seashells
- Trays or bowls
- Water
- Plastic tub
- Paper towels or cardboard
- Pencils or markers
- Clear contact paper or laminator (optional)
- 2 outdoor thermometers

DISCUSSION

The sun is a very powerful energy source. Ask the children if they have ever played outside on a sunny day and ended up with a sunburn. Explain that the sun sends out damaging rays called ultraviolet rays, so we need to apply sunscreen to our bodies to protect our skin. Sunscreen is a lotion or spray that keeps the sun's rays from burning our skin. We can also wear hats to protect our faces and sunglasses to keep the sun out of our eyes.

In this activity, you will use the power of the sun to make prints that are similar to photographs. The sun will create the image of an item on special light-sensitive paper.

ACTIVITY

1. Obtain sun-sensitive paper from a school-supply or art store. Alternatively, you can use dark blue construction paper; however, the sun-sensitive paper works best.
2. Give each child a piece of sun-sensitive paper, a marker or pencil, and some tiny items on a tray or in a little bowl. Ask the children to write their names on their papers.
3. Instruct the children to arrange the small items on the piece of paper in any way they choose. When they are satisfied with their arrangements, they can carefully place the papers in a very sunny place.

4. Wait for the sun to make the prints, which will take five to eight minutes. While you wait, ask the children to experience the heat of the sun. Show them how to use their hands cupped over their eyes to shade themselves from the sun. You can also make shadows with the sun while you are waiting.

5. After five to eight minutes, let the children check on their papers. Have each child carefully lift one item to see if the image appears on the paper. If not, the child should replace the item in the exact same spot. If the image is clear, the child can remove all of the items.

6. Take the prints inside, and keep them out of the sun.

7. Have the children submerge their prints in water in a plastic tub, leaving them underwater for one to five minutes. Set the prints on paper towels or cardboard to dry.

8. If you like, you can laminate the prints for the children, which will help keep the paper from fading further.

LITERACY EXTENSION

Have the children brainstorm their favorite summertime activities. Give each child a chance to draw a picture and write a sentence explaining his summer-sun activity.

Write the words *sun* and *hot* on the board. Have the children help you find rhyming words for each.

- sun—fun, bun, nun, pun, run
- hot—dot, got, lot, not, pot, tot

Exploring Mirrors, Light, and Reflection

CONCEPTS

Exploring reflections, the children will learn the role that light plays. They will learn how a mirror works and will create designs that will be reflected into a mirror.

MATERIALS

For each child or pair of children:

- 2 pieces of mirrored paper or a hinged unbreakable mirror
- Tape
- 2 pieces of white card stock
- Paper
- Pattern-block shapes
- Pencil or marker

DISCUSSION

Ask the children what they see when they look into a mirror. Tell them that they can see themselves because light shining into a mirror bounces back and creates a reflection. When you put two mirrors facing each other, the light bounces back and forth between them.

ACTIVITY

1. If you are creating the hinged mirrors yourself with mirrored paper and card stock, tape the mirrored paper to the card stock and then tape two pieces together to create a hinged mirror. If you are using unbreakable mirrors, then simply tape two together to create a hinged unit for each child or pair of children. Pass out the hinged mirrors.

2. Ask the children to set each hinged mirror on top of a piece of card stock paper, with the hinge positioned to the back.

3. On the edge of the paper farthest away from the mirror hinge, the child should mark a dot and then draw a line from the dot to the mirror hinge. The child should then mark an X on the line between the dot and the hinge. For younger children, the teacher can make the markings on the paper.

4. Let the pairs of children take turns picking up a shape, placing it on the X, and then slowly pushing the shape along the line toward the mirror. If the child looks in the mirror while moving the shape, she will see the shape multiply in the reflection.

5. Ask the children to describe how many shapes they see reflected.

6. As you continue the activity, allow the children to explore using many shapes to make patterns and kaleidoscope effects in their mirrors.

7. Talk with the children about why they see more than one image of the pattern block. Each mirror reflects the light as it bounces from the other mirror. The light keeps bouncing back and forth between the two mirrors, creating images of the pattern blocks.

Playing with Light and Shadows

CONCEPTS

Children are fascinated by shadows. They love to make shadow puppets with their hands. In this activity, they will expand on that idea as they explore new ways to create shadows using light reflected by a mirror.

MATERIALS

For each child or pair of children:

- Hinged, unbreakable mirror or the mirror created in the Exploring Mirrors, Light, and Reflection activity
- Paper
- Small flashlight
- Translucent, colored pattern blocks or pieces of colored cellophane

DISCUSSION

When you use a flashlight, if you hold your fingers in front of it, the light is blocked and a shadow is produced. Light can reflect off a mirror to cast shadows on objects behind the flashlight. The light shines from the flashlight in the mirror, bounces off the mirror, and back toward the flashlight and whatever is behind it. You can block that light bouncing off the mirror to create shadows.

ACTIVITY

1. Give each child a tiny flashlight, an unbreakable hinged mirror, and a piece of paper. If you used the mirrored paper in the Exploring Mirrors, Light, and Reflection activity, you can reuse that mirror setup. Let them set the mirror on the paper, with the hinge pointing toward the back.
2. Dim the lights, and let the children explore what happens when they block the flashlight with their fingers and cast shadows on the paper.
3. Let them explore what happens when they shine light on the mirror. Caution them not to shine the light directly into their eyes. When a child shines the light right into his mirror, the light will bounce off and will appear on his clothes.

4. Give the children translucent, colored pattern-block shapes or pieces of colored cellophane. As they shine the light through the colors, the color will be reflected onto the white paper. Encourage free exploration by suggesting the children try putting two colors on top of each other before shining the light. They will be amazed to see that combining a red shape and a yellow shape will cast an orange shadow.

5. When finished, place the mirrors in your discovery area for continued free exploration.

Cool Vibrations: Sensing Sound Waves

CONCEPTS

In this activity, the children will explore their sense of sound. They will use a tuning fork to hear sound, and they will see and feel the vibrations.

MATERIALS

- Tuning fork
- Water
- Plastic container
- Piece of paper
- Plastic potato toy with body parts, such as Mr. or Mrs. Potato Head

DISCUSSION

Before you begin your discussion, consider that sound travels in the form of vibrations or waves. A vibration is a repeated back-and-forth motion. Vibrating objects make the air around them vibrate. These sound vibrations pass through the air to our ears, strike our eardrums, and cause them to vibrate. Bones in the middle ear transfer the vibrations of the eardrum to the fluid-filled inner ear. The movement of the fluid in the inner ear causes hairlike nerve receptors in the inner ear to move. These receptors carry the message to the brain, and the brain perceives these signals as sound. Although sound can travel through all different types of material, it travels better through some than others.

Beginning the discussion with the children, hold up the toy plastic potato head (be sure the body parts are not on the toy yet), and have a conversation along the following lines. "Here I have a friend. Do you know what her name is? Well, Mrs. Potato Head has body parts that help her from day to day. We all have senses,

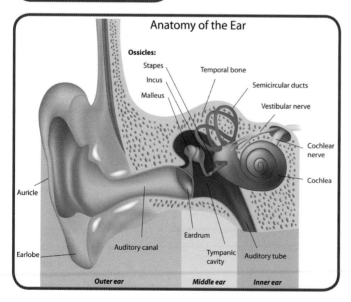

Anatomy of the Ear

Ossicles:
- Stapes
- Incus
- Malleus

Temporal bone
Semicircular ducts
Vestibular nerve
Cochlear nerve
Cochlea

Auricle
Earlobe
Auditory canal
Eardrum
Tympanic cavity
Auditory tube

Outer ear · Middle ear · Inner ear

and certain body parts help us." Then, pick up the eyes, and ask the children to tell you what they are and what they do. When the children respond that the eyes help us see, explain that seeing is one of our senses. Next, pick up the nose and follow the same line of questioning. Discuss that our nose helps with our sense of smell. Continue with the mouth and the sense of taste, the ears and the sense of hearing, and the hands and the sense of touch.

Explain that today they are going to learn more about their sense of hearing. Explain that sound travels in vibrations.

ACTIVITY

1. Introduce the children to the tuning fork. Hold it by the handle end, and strike it on the table so that it begins to vibrate. Once the tuning fork is vibrating, walk around the room and place it next to the ear of each child so that they can all hear the sound. You might have to strike it more than once for everyone to have a chance to hear. Remember, if you touch the child or anything else with the tuning fork, the vibration and sound will stop.

2. Strike the tuning fork again. This time, have the children put out their hands. Touch the vibrating tuning fork to their hands so that they can feel the vibrations. Warn them in advance that the vibration will feel like a little tickle. The tuning fork will stop vibrating each time the end is touched, so you will need to strike it for each child to feel the vibrations.

3. After each child has felt the vibrations, take out a piece of paper, strike the tuning fork on the table, and touch the end of the fork lightly to the piece of paper. Run it up and down the paper, and you will hear a buzzing sound as the tuning fork vibrates on the paper.

4. Finally, strike the tuning fork, and touch the end gently to the top of a container of water. You may need to do this many times to get it to work. Ideally, the vibration will make the water splash.

5

Growing, Adapting, and Exploring Nature

Children get excited when they explore nature and growth and then begin to notice changes in the world around them. Observing how a plant starts as a seed and produces leaves and flowers thrills them. Learning how their bodies work, from the air they breathe to the way exercise helps their hearts pump blood, also can provide stimulating information. They can easily relate to learning about their bodies. Learning about animals is also a never-ending source of fascination for children.

You can capture their attention and empower them by planning activities that explore the way their bodies and the world around them can continually transform and adapt.

Growth and Change: Mealworms

MATERIALS

- Mealworms, available from pet stores or online from sites such as Petco.com or Carolina Biological Supply, www. Carolina.com
- Plastic container
- Oatmeal
- Small sponge
- Photo of yourself as a child
- Diagrams of the life cycles of frogs or butterflies
- Clear plastic cups (optional)
- Bug viewers (optional)
- Test tubes (optional)

For each child:
- Hand lens
- Paper plate
- Paper
- Markers or crayons
- Ruler

CONCEPTS

The children will learn about life cycles and how mealworms grow and change into beetles. They will also learn how to use a hand lens as they closely examine mealworms.

DISCUSSION

All living things grow and change. Explain that when children are born, they are little babies who cannot walk or talk. Further explain that as babies grow, they change. They not only get bigger but also learn to do new things. Ask the children to think of some things that babies do and some things that they can do as older children. Show the children a photo of yourself, and ask a child to tell you how you have changed. Explain that one day they will grow even bigger and be adults. Show images or diagrams of the life cycles of frogs and butterflies as examples of how animals grow and change.

Tell the children that mealworms start out as tiny eggs and turn into beetles. Like a caterpillar, mealworms go into a sort of sleeping state called a pupa. When they wake up and come out of the pupa, they will turn into black beetles. Mealworms can be found in dark and dry places. They are scavengers and like to eat grain and cereal.

For older children, you can go into more detail, telling them that mealworms have a four-stage life cycle. They begin as eggs about as tiny as a dot you can make with the point of a pencil. The second stage is the larva or mealworm stage. Next, the mealworm begins its metamorphosis and becomes a sleepy pupa. In the adult stage, it becomes a black beetle.

ACTIVITY

1. Purchase mealworms from a pet store, and house them in a plastic container with air holes. Fill the container about half full with oatmeal, and add a small piece of wet sponge. The environment should be dry, not moist.

2. Give each child a paper plate on which you have placed two mealworms. Give the children hand lenses, and invite them to observe the mealworms.

3. Explain to the children that mealworms do not bite and cannot hurt them. Also remind them that they are living things and that we have to be gentle with them.

4. Some children enjoy taking the mealworms out of the container of oatmeal, while others will be scared. Those who are scared can view the mealworms in a clear cup, bug viewer, or test tube. Viewing in a clear container also helps the children get a better look at the legs and underside.

5. Once the children get used to handling the mealworms, the critters can make a great addition to your discovery area or learning station for free exploration.

6. Ask the children to draw their mealworms. They can name their specimens and can measure them. Have them write down the measurements in millimeters.

7. Older children can use the hand lens to get a closer look at the mealworm. Ask them to look for eyes, legs, mouth parts, and hair.

8. For further scientific exploration and writing exercises, ask the older children to do these activities, writing down their answers.

   - Gently blow on the mealworm, and write a sentence telling how it responded.
   - Tap on the table next to the mealworm. Did it walk away or stay near the tapping sound?
   - What senses did you use to observe your mealworm?
   - Name the four stages that a mealworm goes through.

MINDING THE MATH

Have the children explore number-related activities and write down their findings.

- Count how many mealworms are in the big container.
- Measure two mealworms, and compare the sizes.
- Count the number of legs on each mealworm.
- Think of five things that are longer than your mealworm and five things that are shorter.

Animal Adaptations: Marine Mammals and Blubber

CONCEPTS

The children will learn about mammals and how marine mammals use their thick blubber to stay warm in water. Through discussion, the children will learn about comparing attributes or characteristics. They will also review the concepts of hot and cold.

MATERIALS

- Yardstick or ruler
- Bucket or bowl
- Ice
- Water
- Plastic spoons
- Shortening
- Rubber gloves, one for each child
- Paper towels
- Whiteboard or chart paper
- Marker

DISCUSSION

Begin by talking about how children can be grouped as boys or girls. Note that animals are also divided into groups by their characteristics. Compare and contrast different types of animals so that the children understand that mammals have hair or fur, are warm blooded, and have lungs to breathe like humans do. Explain that marine mammals are mammals that live in the water. Some examples include whales, dolphins, seals, walruses, and manatees.

Most marine mammals have smooth, rubbery skin that helps them slip easily through the water. To keep warm, their bodies have layers of blubber. Blubber is the thick layer of fat that the animals use to conserve body heat. If a mammal's food source is hard to find, it can live off of its blubber for a long time. Blubber is lighter than water, so it increases buoyancy in marine mammals and helps them float.

Have each child grab a little pinch of skin at his wrist. Explain that between their skin and bones is fat, which helps keep them warm. Discuss that the small amount of fat they feel under their skin is less than an inch. Use a yardstick to show them an inch. For comparison, tell them that marine mammals can have between 6 and 20 inches of blubber to keep them warm. Explain that in this activity they are going to pretend that they are marine mammals and find out how their blubber keeps them warm.

ACTIVITY

1. Ahead of time, fill a bucket with water and ice.
2. Explain that the children will have shortening to simulate blubber on the fingers of one hand and that they will experiment to see which fingers feel warmer: the ones with the blubber or the ones without. Ask the children to predict which fingers will stay warmer. Make a tally of the predictions on the board.
3. Bring small groups of children at a time up to the bucket of ice water that you have prepared. As a child comes up to participate, place a rubber glove on one of her hands. Hold her hand out flat, and spread the shortening on the gloved fingers.
4. Ask her to hold those fingers together and place both hands in the ice water. Count off fifteen seconds, and then the child can pull her hand out and take off the glove. Hand her a paper towel to use to clean or dry her hand if necessary.
5. Discuss with the children which fingers felt colder: the ones with blubber or the ones without. They should respond that the fingers without the shortening felt colder. Then, ask which fingers felt warmer.
6. Compare the predictions with the outcome, and discuss the findings.

MINDING THE MATH

Count how many children predicted the hand with the shortening would be warmer. Compare that number to the results. You can also use a thermometer to measure the temperature of the water, which will be about zero Celsius. Compare that to the temperature of water at room temperature.

Comparing Different Animal Homes

The children will learn that animals are adapted to living in different types of environments. After listing different animal homes, they will take part in making a simulated spiderweb.

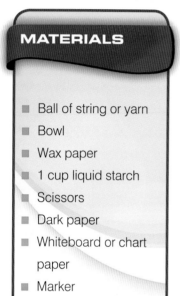

MATERIALS

- Ball of string or yarn
- Bowl
- Wax paper
- 1 cup liquid starch
- Scissors
- Dark paper
- Whiteboard or chart paper
- Marker

DISCUSSION

All living things are adapted or equipped to thrive in specific environments. Some prefer to live in hot environments, and others prefer cold ones. Some animals are adapted to live in the water, and others to live on land. Animals also are adapted to living in different homes. Draw the following table on the board, and have the children help fill in the animal homes. (The answers have been provided for you. Do not list them on the board; rather, engage the children in coming up with the appropriate responses.)

ANIMALS AND THEIR HOMES

Animal	Home
Ant	Anthill
Wasp	Hive
Turtle	Shell
Crab	Shell
Bear	Den
Fish	Water
Bee	Hive
Bird	Nest
Spider	Web
Snail	Shell
Gopher	Underground

Explain that a spider is adapted to living in a web. The spider has spinnerets that release strands, which it weaves together to make the web. Some of the strands are coated with sticky substances to trap the prey so the spider can capture it. Explain that in this activity, you will be making a spiderweb.

ACTIVITY

1. Pour 1 cup of liquid starch into a bowl.
2. Cut four pieces of string or yarn into 7-inch lengths.
3. Lay out a piece of wax paper, and pass out 7-inch pieces of string to four children. Have the children take turns dipping their entire piece of string in the liquid starch.
4. Lay down the first two pieces so that they make a plus sign on the wax paper.
5. The next two children should lay down their strings in the spaces between the other ones, intersecting at the center to form a large asterisk.
6. Soak the rest of the ball of string in the liquid starch.
7. With a continuous piece of string, have the children connect the ends of the 7-inch pieces to form the outside of the web and then move inward in a spiral design.
8. Allow the web to dry overnight. Remove it from the wax paper once it is completely dry, and tape it to a window or dark surface.

MINDING THE MATH

Take a walking tour around the school, and look for spiderwebs to get a closer look. Count how many spiderwebs are found around the school. Remind the children that they should not touch an animal they see in the wild, unless an adult says it is safe.

LITERACY EXTENSION

Help the children write animal words, such as *tiger* or *ladybug*, on cards. Have them count how many letters are in the word and write the number on the card. Put the words in order from the least to the most letters.

You can also see if the children can find an animal or insect to go with each letter of the alphabet. Here are some examples: *A* is for ant; *B* is for bear; *C* is for cat; *D* is for dog; *E* is for elephant; *F* is for frog; *G* is for gorilla; *H* is for hippo; *I* is for iguana; *J* is for jackrabbit; *K* is for kangaroo; *L* is for lion; *M* is for moose; *N* is for newt; *O* is for octopus; *P* is for pig; *Q* is for quail; *R* is for rooster; *S* is for sheep; *T* is for turtle; *U* is for urchin; *V* is for vulture; *W* is for walrus; *X* is for X-ray fish; *Y* is for yak; *Z* is for zebra.

Understanding Air and Blowing Bubbles

CONCEPTS

The children will learn that air is all around us and that we need air to breathe. They will also learn that air has weight and takes up space.

MATERIALS

■ Tape measure or ruler

For each child:
● Bubble solution
● Small tray
● Drinking straw

DISCUSSION

Explain to the children that air is all around us. We cannot see air because it is a gas. We can see when things outside blow back and forth because wind is moving air. Most living things need air to survive. Humans have lungs inside their bodies that assist with breathing. When we breathe, we inhale (breathe in) air, called oxygen, into our lungs. We exhale (breathe out) another gas called carbon dioxide.

Demonstrate, and have each child place his hand on his chest. Instruct the children to take a deep breath in and then exhale. Point out how their chests move up and down as they inhale and exhale. You can also discuss the concept of inflating a balloon. We exhale air into the balloon. That air takes up space. We can see that when the balloon grows from the air.

ACTIVITY

1. Pass out a small tray and a straw to each child. Pour about 2 tablespoons of the bubble solution on each tray.

2. Have the children practice blowing air into the straw. They can feel the air coming out the end by placing their hands at the other ends of their straws. Explain the difference between inhaling and exhaling. When

you drink out of a straw, you draw the beverage into the straw. When you exhale, you are blowing out. For this activity, it is important that the children only exhale so that they will not drink the soap! As a precaution, you can cut a small hole about a third of the way down the straw so the children will not be able to inhale the solution.

3. Demonstrate placing the straw in the bubble solution on the tray. Gently blow, and watch as the bubble grows in size.

4. Children who are having difficulty can be shown how to stir the bubble solution with the end of the straw to make teeny tiny bubbles. By placing the straw inside the tiny bubbles, they can blow softly to make them bigger. Once they get the hang of making one bubble, challenge the children to see how many bubbles they can make on their trays. The key to blowing great bubbles is to blow gently.

MINDING THE MATH

Have the children count how many bubbles they can make on one tray before the bubbles pop. You can also use a tape measure to measure the bubble once it pops. When the bubble pops, it will leave a wet ring behind that can be easily measured. Older children can graph the number of bubbles as well as the bubble size.

Our Hearts and Circulation: A Matter of Exercise

CONCEPTS

The children will learn about the heart and the role it plays in circulation. They will do various activities and will learn how to feel their pulses to determine which activities are most strenuous for the heart. They will also practice counting and will review the concept of time.

- Large, open space, preferably outside
- Chart paper or whiteboard
- Stopwatch
- Stethoscope (optional)

DISCUSSION

The heart is one of the most powerful muscles in the body. Explain that your heart is inside your chest. Place your own hand over your heart to demonstrate where the heart is located. As a person grows, his heart also grows. A human heart is about the size of a fist. Pulse is a measure of a heartbeat; each throb of the pulse represents one beat of the heart. The heart pumps blood throughout the circulatory system of veins, arteries, and capillaries. Every second, the heart pumps 70 milliliters of blood. The total number of throbs in one minute is called the pulse rate. When you go to the doctor's office, the doctor sometimes uses a stethoscope to hear your heart beating. (If you have a stethoscope, let the children listen to their own heartbeats.) Explain that the more strenuous or harder a physical activity is, the faster the heart will beat. Ask the children to predict which of the following activities will be the most strenuous for the heart: jumping jacks, or jogging or dancing in place.

ACTIVITY

1. Prepare the paper or whiteboard with two columns, one labeled *Jogging or Dancing,* and one labeled *Jumping Jacks.*

2. Demonstrate that you can feel your pulse by sitting very still and placing your index and middle fingers together and holding them on your neck just under your jaw. At first, the children may have difficulty finding their pulses because the heart does not work very hard when someone is sitting still. After doing some exercise, they will be able to find their pulses more easily.

3. Put on some music, and tell the children to dance or jog to the music for one minute. Explain that after one minute you will tell them to sit very still and find their pulses. Use a stopwatch to time the children.

4. After a minute of dancing or jogging in place, call out, "Stop and sit very still, and find your pulse."

5. When all the children are sitting with their fingers on their necks, tell them to begin counting how many times they feel their pulse moving. With the stopwatch, time them for ten seconds. At the end of the ten seconds, tell them to stop and remember their numbers.

6. Ask each child to report her number, and write the numbers on the paper or whiteboard. You would normally multiply this number by six to get the pulse rate per minute, but for this activity you can compare the ten-second rate for the two different activities.

7. Repeat this activity with jumping jacks, and compare which activity is the most strenuous for the heart.

MINDING THE MATH

Make two columns on the board, one for dancing or jogging and the other for jumping jacks. In each column, write down the ten-second pulse rate for each child for that activity. Have the children identify the lowest number and the highest number in each column.

LITERACY EXTENSION

Write the word *heart* on the board. Have each child draw a picture of herself and label where her heart would be in her body. Ask the children to identify the first letter in the word *heart*. Have an *h* hunt. See how many words the children can come up with that start with the letter *h*.

Examining Seeds and Observing Growth

CONCEPTS

The children will learn that, like an animal, a plant follows a life cycle as it develops. Children will use a hand lens to examine dry and soaked seeds. They will describe the physical properties, comparing the sizes and shapes. They will remove the seed coat to reveal the new plant. They will begin a study of plants and gardening by planting their seeds.

MATERIALS

- Seedling vegetable plant in a container
- Water
- Tape

For each child:
- Paper towel
- 2 lima beans soaked in water overnight
- 1 dry lima bean
- Hand lens
- Ruler (optional for younger children)
- Plastic sandwich bag or cup

For each child (estimation activity):
- Paper cup
- Several dry lima beans
- Paper clips

DISCUSSION

Note that all living things grow and change. When the children were born, they were tiny babies, and now they have grown and developed into youngsters. The same is true with plants. At this point, show the seedling vegetable plant to the children. Tell them that the plant did not always look like this; it started from a tiny seed. The seed went through changes and grew to become a plant.

Seeds are alike in many ways. They develop in the ovary of a plant and contain a little plant called an embryo. Seeds are covered by a thin outer coating called a seed coat, which protects the seed. The tiny seed has its own food until it is able to make food in its leaves. A bean seed is a dicotyledon, meaning it has two cotyledons, or food storage areas. The embryo is found between the two cotyledons.

ACTIVITY

1. Pass out a paper towel, a hand lens, two soaked seeds, and one dry seed to each child.

2. Have the children look at the dry and soaked seeds without using their hand lenses. Ask them to tell how the seeds are alike and different.

3. On the board draw the table, and ask the children to tell you some physical properties of the seeds, such as size, shape, texture, and color. Write their responses in the appropriate columns.

PHYSICAL PROPERTIES OF SEEDS OBSERVED	
Dry Seed	Soaked Seed

Possible responses for the properties of the dry seeds are that they are dry, smaller, white, hard, and smooth. Possible responses for the properties of the soaked seeds are that they are wet, bigger, wrinkled, soft, and white.

4. Instruct the children to use a hand lens to get a closer look at each soaked seed. Show them how to remove the seed coat, and give them a chance to peel it off each seed.

5. Demonstrate opening the seed, and see if they can find the tiny plant inside. If you use the hand lens, when the tiny plant falls out you can actually see a tiny leaf. The leaf will be white unless it has been soaking a few days. If it has, then it will be green.

6. Use the dry seeds to have the children work in pairs to grow plants. Ask each pair to fold a paper towel into a square and wet it. Have them place the paper towel in a sandwich bag or plastic cup and drop in two lima beans. They can tape the bag to the window and observe what happens.

7. Periodically take each bag down, and measure the plant that is growing inside. Be sure to leave the bag open at the top so that the plant can grow out of the bag.

8. Make a chart, and each day write the day and what the class has observed about their plants.

9. Older children can do their own growth journals, measuring the plants themselves. They can also draw what happens.

10. Resist the urge to send these plants home. Once they have grown a bit and leaves have formed, transplant them into cups of soil.

11. When the plants are hardy enough, transplant them into a garden for the children. If you are patient and water them well, they will come full circle and will grow new lima beans.

MINDING THE MATH

Give each child a small paper cup with beans. Have the children estimate how many beans are in the cup. Next, lay the beans out, and count them to confirm the answers. Use paper clips as a nonstandard measure, and find the length of the line of beans.

LITERACY EXTENSION

Older children can keep a journal and make daily observations with words and illustrations describing the growth of their seeds.

Pumpkin Properties and Predictions

CONCEPTS

The children will examine a pumpkin inside and out, measuring and weighing it and counting the number of seeds inside. They will review the concepts of sinking and floating and will predict whether or not their pumpkins will float when placed in water.

DISCUSSION

Pumpkins are fruits that grow on leafy vines and start as seeds. Yellow-orange flowers bloom on the vine, and then they die and wither away. The flowers' ovaries (at the bottom of the flower) swell and become tiny green pumpkins. As they grow larger, they change color. About four months after planting the seeds, you can harvest your pumpkins, which contain vitamin A and potassium. The colors vary; they could be white, yellow, or orange. Pumpkins are used in pies, breads, soups, and other recipes, and are sometimes used to feed farm animals. Pumpkin seeds can be roasted for a snack.

ACTIVITY

1. Ahead of time, fill a large bowl or bucket with water. Fill a small garbage can with water.
2. Show the children a small pumpkin, and have them predict whether it will sink or float when dropped in water. Count how many children predict that it will sink and how many predict that it will float. Introduce the concept of a tally, and tally the predictions on the board.
3. Place one of the tiny pumpkins into the water in the bucket. Discuss what happens. Some children might think that even though the little one floats, the bigger

pumpkin will sink. Be prepared to test that one as well. You can fill a small garbage can with water to test the big one.

4. On the board or chart paper, draw the tables and graphs that follow, and use them to record the children's findings in their pumpkin investigations.

5. Show the children the tape measure, and demonstrate how to use it to measure around the big pumpkin. Tell them that the distance around something is the circumference.

6. If you have a few little pumpkins, each child can measure the distance around one of them. The children can work in groups, with one child holding the pumpkin in the air and a different one measuring it. Record the children's findings on a chart like the one shown, Record Pumpkin Circumference, or graph their findings (see next page).

7. The children can also measure across the tops of the pumpkins to determine the diameter of each. Record their findings on a chart like the one shown, Record Pumpkin Diameter, or graph their findings (see next page).

8. The children can also count the number of lines on each pumpkin. Record their findings on a chart like the one on page 128, Record Pumpkin Lines, or on a graph like the one on page 128, Graph Pumpkin Lines.

9. Let the children predict the number of seeds in the pumpkins. Afterward, you can use the knife to cut the pumpkins open and gather the seeds. Put the seeds on paper plates, and have the children count the seeds. Bigger pumpkins have more seeds. You can have the children make assumptions about the number of seeds after cutting into the little ones to see if they think the bigger one will have more seeds.

RECORD PUMPKIN CIRCUMFERENCE

Pumpkin	Number of Inches Around
P1	
P2	
P3	
P4	
P5	

RECORD PUMPKIN DIAMETER

Pumpkin	Number of Inches Across
P1	
P2	
P3	
P4	
P5	

GRAPH PUMPKIN CIRCUMFERENCE

Number of Inches Around		P1	P2	P3	P4	P5
	9					
	8					
	7					
	6					
	5					
	4					
	3					
	2					
	1					
		P1	P2	P3	P4	P5
				Pumpkin		

GRAPH PUMPKIN DIAMETER

Number of Inches Across		P1	P2	P3	P4	P5
	9					
	8					
	7					
	6					
	5					
	4					
	3					
	2					
	1					
		P1	P2	P3	P4	P5
				Pumpkin		

RECORD PUMPKIN LINES

Pumpkin	Number of Lines
P1	
P2	
P3	
P4	
P5	

GRAPH PUMPKIN LINES

Number of Lines		P1	P2	P3	P4	P5
	9					
	8					
	7					
	6					
	5					
	4					
	3					
	2					
	1					
		P1	P2	P3	P4	P5

Pumpkin

MINDING THE MATH

Make a T chart, and record the children's predictions of how many seeds they will find in their pumpkins. Then, let them count the seeds. Compare their predictions with the actual number of seeds that they find.

LITERACY EXTENSION

Have the children draw pumpkins and illustrate how their families might carve them for Halloween or a fall festival. Let them write or dictate a story explaining how they might use their pumpkins.

Planting and Harvesting Radishes

CONCEPTS

Gardening can be another way to encourage scientific discovery and mathematical thinking. The children will experience planting radish seeds and growing them into vegetable plants. Once the radishes are grown and harvested, they can compare sizes, count the radishes, and even cut them and taste how bitter they are. Variations include growing peppers, cabbages, lettuce, herbs, cucumbers, squash, or eggplants.

Each type of plant provides opportunities for observation and measurement.

MATERIALS

- Packet of about 100 radish seeds
- Wooden craft sticks
- Soil
- Water
- Rulers
- Cups (optional)
- Rubber balls (optional)
- Balance scale (optional)

DISCUSSION

Begin by talking about the food the children had for lunch the day before. Ask them if they know where the food came from—for example, the milk came from a cow, the meat from a chicken, the fruit from trees, and the vegetables from the ground. Review the life cycle of the lima bean seed as it becomes a plant. Let them know that they will plant a tiny radish seed and that it will produce an actual radish. Ask if they have tasted a radish before. Ask those who have not tasted one to predict whether it will be sweet, sour, or bitter. You may want to discuss those words and provide examples of sweet, sour, and bitter foods.

ACTIVITY

1. Give each child a wooden craft stick and a cup of soil. Have them use the sticks to poke holes in their cups of soil. Alternatively, you can do this activity outside in a garden.

2. Give each child one or two seeds, and let the children plant their seeds in the holes they created in the soil. After the children put the seeds in, they should gently cover them with soil.

3. Encourage the children to observe the plants often. Water them as needed to keep the soil moist. Have the children track how many plants are growing and measure how tall they are.

4. In addition to taking measurements, invite the children to draw pictures of the things they observe in the garden. Assist in labeling the drawings as needed.

5. When you harvest the radishes, perhaps you can use a nonstandard measurement such as a small rubber bouncing ball. Have the children graph whether the radishes are smaller, the same size, or larger than the ball.

6. With older children, you can extend the activity using a balance scale for weighing. Have the children pile radishes into a container and put them on one side of the scale. Ask the children to put blocks on the other side until they balance the weight. Have them count how many radishes and how many blocks equal the same weight.

7. Give the children harvested vegetables to take home. You may find that the children will eat more vegetables! They are apt to try what they have grown, picked, and packed to take home. These activities can improve nutritional awareness and healthy eating.

Hands-On Science and Math

ADDITIONAL GARDENING ACTIVITIES USING SCIENCE AND MATH

Because there are many different ways to approach gardening, evaluate the space you have to work with. If you can devote a small outdoor area to a garden, you can plant in containers, beds of soil, or even right outside your classroom. You can also use concrete blocks to make gardening beds. Set up the blocks in a rectangular shape, and dump soil inside the rectangular area. You can even plant in the holes of the blocks. One strategy is to plant seedlings in the center of the bed and marigolds in the holes of the blocks. The marigolds will act as a natural pesticide.

If you do not have access to water or a hose, consider hooking up your gutter to a rain barrel and recycling the rainwater. You can keep little watering cans by the rain barrel for the children to use for water, or hook up a hose directly to the barrel. Frequent watering is essential for the success of your garden.

Using seedling plants can cut down your growing time and give you better success than starting with seeds alone. You can purchase seedlings at stores with garden departments. To plant seedlings, make holes in the garden bed or container, remove the plants from their packaging, place them in the ground, and spread the dirt to fill in the hole.

When measuring in the garden, you can use a tape measure or paper clips, snapping cubes, or craft sticks as nonstandard measures.

More ideas for planting seedlings and harvesting the results:

- **Cherry tomatoes:** As they grow, children can chart their growth, measure the height of the plant, and count the number of flowers and then tomatoes. Put the tomatoes on a balance scale to find the weight, or use the tomatoes for estimation. You can put the tomatoes in a salad, or let the children pop them in their mouths and eat them!
- **Cabbages:** When the cabbages are grown, the children can count the leaves on each head. They can also use a tape measure to measure across or around the cabbage heads.
- **Bell and banana peppers:** Compare the colors, and measure the length of and distance around the peppers.
- **Cauliflower:** Use a tape measure to measure across the cauliflower.
- **Broccoli:** As the plant grows, measure the height with a tape measure.

Children also love drawing and painting pictures of vegetables in the garden.

Junior Geologists: Rock Quest

CONCEPTS

The children will learn that a geologist is a scientist who studies rocks. This activity will give the children an opportunity to explore rocks, compare and contrast rock sizes and colors, and use a hand lens to get a closer look.

MATERIALS

- Plastic shoe boxes with lids (2 or 3 children can share)
- Sand
- Different types of rocks
- Balance scale (optional)

DISCUSSION

Explain to the children that paleontologists are scientists who study fossils, and geologists are scientists who study rocks. Tell the children that they can be geologists for a day as they search through boxes of sand to uncover rock samples.

ACTIVITY

1. Fill each plastic shoe box with sand. Hide a variety of rocks in the sand for the children to discover.
2. Divide the children into pairs or groups of three. Give each group a shoe box, and remove the lid, placing it next to the plastic box. Let the children take turns sifting through the sand. They can place any rocks they find on the plastic lids.
3. Once they have found all the rocks, ask the children to place the lids back on their boxes with the rocks on top. This will keep the children from playing in the sand (which they can do another time) and will concentrate their attention on the lids filled with rocks.
4. Have the children count the rocks; view them with hand lenses; and compare the rocks by color, size, and shape.

5. Following the activity, go on a rock hunt, or encourage the children to look for rocks during the course of the week at home and at parks. Set up a place in the classroom where the children can display those rocks and compare them with the rocks you have provided. Your discovery area is a great place to keep rock collections.

MINDING THE MATH

Use a balance scale to compare the weights of rocks. For younger children, give them two rocks, and ask them to predict which is heavier. Check their predictions by placing one rock on each side of a balance scale to see which is heaviest. Also, place rocks in a container, and have the children arrange them in size from smallest to largest. Older children can actually weigh the rocks on a balance scale using items such as wood blocks or metal washers to balance the scale. They can also number the rocks and graph the weight of each one.

Promoting Free Exploration

As you finish an activity in this book, you and the children are ready for a new beginning. You can encourage the children to investigate further by providing math and science activities in the discovery areas in the classroom. You can extend what they learned from an activity by giving them new opportunities to explore using the equipment, supplies, and concepts that are now familiar to them. During directed group activities, you have explained the concepts in advance, led the children through the steps involved, and asked them to reflect and report on their experiences. Now give them free exploration time so that they can exercise their inquiry skills, practice and experiment more on their own, and think critically about the ideas they have encountered. Provide some activities that the children have done before so that they can practice and extend previously learned concepts.

Science learning stations provide great opportunities for free exploration. Think out of the box to come up with items to put in science stations. With donations from families, class stations can include old keys and buttons for sorting, telephone or cable cords for measuring, plastic caps of different colors and sizes for classifying, and so on. Children love to explore mundane items. Rotate materials often, and provide new materials to keep the explorations exciting.

More free exploration ideas:

- Children are amazed with animal tracks. You can purchase molds and make castings with plaster of Paris and paint, or you can use playdough. Place the molds in an exploration station, and let the children make the animal tracks over and over using playdough. If you leave the playdough tracks out, they will get hard.

- Place magnets and items to test in a box.
- Collect nuts, bolts, and other hardware items to count and sort.
- Provide containers of water and items to test to see if they sink or float. On other occasions, take out the sinking and floating items and replace them with containers for dumping and pouring practice. Another time, place test-tube racks with funnels or pipettes for exploration.
- Set out gear sets for experimentation.
- Put hand lenses and items to view in a box. Be sure to include natural specimens such as rocks, shells, feathers, and leaves.
- Have boxes of collections of rocks, shells, or pinecones.

Appendix: Graphing Topics

Graphing is a means of data representation that provides daily opportunities for the children to analyze, count, compare, and contrast. You can come up with an endless supply of daily graphing topics to keep children engaged. Graphing is a way for you to explain the results of an experiment or simply to see how the children feel about things. A graph always answers a question. For example, if you wanted to order pizza but did not know what type to order, you could ask a group of people what kinds they like the best. Then, count up each person's vote, and order the pizza type that the most people like.

You can use a graphing pocket chart and make graphing part of the classroom routine. Choose a topic, and write the question on the top of the graphing pocket chart. Place the choices in the pockets in the bottom of the chart. Give each child either a card with his photo or a slip of paper with his name on it, and call the children up one at a time to cast a vote. After each child has made his choice, count how many children voted for each option. Do not miss the opportunity to create number sentences discussing how many more, how many less, or how much in all.

When graphing is done as a daily habit, children gain concrete examples of using mathematics in their daily lives in a way that is meaningful. Potential graphing topics are endless.

Food Questions

What is your favorite food?

What is your favorite fruit?

What is your favorite green vegetable?

What is your favorite ice-cream flavor?

What is your favorite dessert?

What is your favorite cookie?

What is your favorite snack?

What is your favorite pizza topping?

What taste do you like the best?

How do you like your pizza crust?

What is your favorite milkshake flavor?

What is your favorite breakfast food?

What is your favorite type of berry?

How do you like to eat your eggs?

What is your favorite kind of pie?

Which apple color do you like best?

What is your favorite kind of doughnut?

Which soup do you like best?

What is your favorite milk flavor?

Will you eat a hot or cold lunch today?

Animal Questions

What is your favorite animal?

What is your favorite reptile?

What is your favorite insect?

What is your favorite creepy-crawly?

What is your favorite mammal?

What is your favorite dinosaur?

What kind of dinosaur would you be?

Which is your favorite fish?

Which fish looks the meanest?

What is your favorite pet?

What is your favorite bird?

What is your favorite farm animal?

Do you have a four-legged or two-legged pet?

Questions about the Children

Are you a girl or a boy?

Which word best describes your hair?

What color are your eyes?

What are you wearing today?

How many letters are in your name?

How many sisters and brothers do you have?

How many people live in your house?

Who is your favorite community helper?

Do you use bubbles in your bath?

Does your shirt have buttons or no buttons?

Do your pants have pockets or no pockets?

In which month were you born?

What color socks are you wearing today?

What are your favorite shoes?

What would you like to be when you grow up?

How many teeth have you lost?

How many doors are in your house?

How do you get to school?

How do you feel today?

How many syllables are in your last name?

How many syllables are in your first name?

Do you like sunshine, snow, or rain?

Do you like daytime or nighttime?

Where would you like to go on vacation?

What kind of toothpaste do you like best?

What time did you go to sleep last night?

Do you brush, brush and floss, or neither?

Do you like baths or showers?

Which leaf do you like the best?

Recreation and Hobby Questions

What is your favorite sport?

What is your favorite holiday?

What is your favorite cartoon or movie character?

What is your favorite play area?

What is your favorite stuffed toy?

What is your favorite balloon color?

What is your favorite character?

What is your favorite shape?

What is your favorite way to exercise?

What is your favorite beach activity?

Which medium do you like to use most for art?

Which movie is your favorite?

Who is your favorite superhero?

Resources

Ashbrook, Peggy. 2003. *Science Is Simple: Over 250 Activities for Preschoolers.* Beltsville, MD: Gryphon House.

Benson, Jennifer, and Jennifer Miller. 2008. "Experiences in Nature: A Pathway to Standards." *Young Children* 63(4): 22–28.

Blake, Sally. 2009. "Engage, Investigate, and Report: Enhancing the Curriculum with Scientific Inquiry." *Young Children* 64(6): 49–53.

Bosse, Sherrie, Gera Jacobs, and Tara L. Anderson. 2009. "Science in the Air." *Young Children* 64(6): 10–15.

Brennan, Georgeanne, and Ethel Brennan. 2004. *The Children's Kitchen Garden: A Book of Gardening, Cooking, and Learning.* Berkeley, CA: Ten Speed Press.

Brenneman, Kimberly. 2009. "Let's Find Out! Preschoolers as Scientific Explorers." *Young Children* 64(6): 54–60.

Buchanan, Becky L., and Jose M. Rios. 2004. "Teaching Science to Kindergartners: How Can Teachers Implement Science Standards?" *Young Children* 59(3): 82–87.

Chalufour, Ingrid, and Karen Worth. 2003. *Discovering Nature with Young Children.* St. Paul, MN: Redleaf.

Charlesworth, Rosalind, and Karen K. Lind. 2012. *Math and Science for Young Children.* 7th ed. Belmont, CA: Wadsworth.

Conezio, Kathleen, and Lucia French. 2002. "Science in the Preschool Classroom: Capitalizing on Children's Fascination with the Everyday World to Foster Language and Literacy Development." *Young Children* 57(5): 12–18.

Copple, Carol, and Sue Bredekamp. 2009. *Developmentally Appropriate Practice in Early Childhood Programs Serving Children from Birth through Age 8.* 3rd ed. Washington, DC: National Association for the Education of Young Children (NAEYC).

Cowan, Kay W., and Sandra Cipriani. 2009. "Of Water Troughs and the Sun: Developing Inquiry through Analogy." *Young Children* 64(6): 62–67.

Crawford, Elizabeth, Emily T. Heaton, Karen Heslop, and Kassandra Kixmiller. 2009. "Science Learning at Home: Involving Families." *Young Children* 64(6): 39–41.

Desrochers, Joyce. 2001. "Exploring Our World: Outdoor Classes for Parents and Children." *Young Children* 56(5): 9–11.

Evitt, Marie F., with Tim Dobbins and Bobbi Weesen-Baer. 2009. *Thinking BIG, Learning BIG: Connecting Science, Math, Literacy, and Language in Early Childhood.* Beltsville, MD: Gryphon House.

Farrell, Jill, and Robert Vos, eds. 2007. *Growing Together in Community through Action Research.* Miami, FL: Florida International University Center for Urban Education and Innovation.

French, Lucia. 2004. "Science as the Center of a Coherent, Integrated Early Childhood Curriculum." *Early Childhood Research Quarterly* 19(1): 138–49.

Gelman, Rochel, Kimberly Brenneman, Gay Macdonald, and Moises Roman. 2009. *Preschool Pathways to Science: Facilitating Scientific Ways of Thinking, Talking, and Doing, and Understanding.* Baltimore, MD: Brookes.

Hachey, Alyse C., and Deanna L. Butler. 2009. "Seeds in the Window, Soil in the Sensory Table: Science Education through Gardening and Nature-Based Play." *Young Children* 64(6): 42–48.

Helm, Judy H., and Lilian G. Katz. 2010. *Young Investigators: The Project Approach in the Early Years.* 2nd ed. New York: Teachers College Press.

Howley-Pfeifer, Patricia. 2002. "Raising Butterflies from Your Own Garden." *Young Children* 57(6): 60–65.

Humphryes, Janet. 2000. "Exploring Nature with Children." *Young Children* 55(2): 16–20.

Klein, Evelyn R., Penny L. Hammrich, Stefanie Bloom, and Anika Ragins. 2000. "Language Development and Science Inquiry: The Head Start on Science and Communication Program." *Early Childhood Research and Practice* 2(2). http://ecrp.uiuc.edu/v2n2/klein.html

Koralek, Derry, and Laura Colker, eds. 2003. *Spotlight on Young Children and Science.* Washington, DC: NAEYC.

Korte, Katrina M., Laura Fielden, and Josephine C. Agnew. 2005. "To Run, Stomp, or Study: Hissing Cockroaches in the Classroom." *Young Children* 60(2): 12–18.

Lind, Karen. 2004. "Science in Early Childhood: Developing and Acquiring Fundamental Concepts and Skills." In Dialogue on Early Childhood Science, Mathematics, and Technology Education. Project 2061 series. Washington, DC: American Association for the Advancement of Science.

Louv, Richard. 2008. *Last Child in the Woods: Saving Our Children from Nature-Deficit Disorder.* Chapel Hill, NC: Algonquin.

McHenry, Jolie D., and Kathy J. Buerk. 2008. "Infants and Toddlers Meet the Natural World." *Young Children* 63(1): 40–41.

McNair, Shannan. 2006. *Start Young! Early Childhood Science Activities.* Arlington, VA: National Science Teachers Association Press.

Mohrmann, Pam. 1999. "Planting the Seeds of Science: The School Garden—A Perfect Laboratory for Teaching Science." *Instructor* 108(16): 25–29.

Moriarty, Robin F. 2002. "Entries from a Staff Developer's Journal . . . Helping Teachers Develop as Facilitators of Three- to Five-Year-Olds' Science Inquiry." *Young Children* 57(5): 20–24.

National Arbor Day Foundation and Dimensions Educational Research Foundation. 2007. *Learning with Nature Idea Book: Creating Nurturing Outdoor Spaces for Children.* Lincoln, NE: National Arbor Day Foundation.

National Research Council. 2000. *Inquiry and the National Science Education Standards: A Guide for Teaching and Learning.* Washington, DC: National Academies Press.

National Research Council. 2005. *Mathematical and Scientific Development in Early Childhood: A Workshop Summary.* Washington, DC: National Academies Press.

National Research Council. 2007. *Ready, Set, Science! Putting Research to Work in K-8 Science Classrooms.* Washington, DC: National Academies Press.

Neuman, Susan, and Kathleen Roskos, with Tanya Wright and Lisa Lenhart. 2007. *Nurturing Knowledge: Building a Foundation for School Success by Linking Early Literacy to Math, Science, Art, and Social Studies.* New York: Scholastic.

Nimmo, John, and Beth Hallett. 2008. "Childhood in the Garden: A Place to Encounter Natural and Social Diversity." *Young Children* 63(1): 32–38.

Ozer, Emily J. 2007. "The Effects of School Gardens on Students and Schools: Conceptualization and Considerations for Maximizing Healthy Development." *Health Education & Behavior* 34(6): 846–63.

Patrick, Helen, Panayota Mantzicopoulos, and Ala Samarapungavan. 2009. "Reading, Writing, and Conducting Inquiry about Science in Kindergarten." *Young Children* 64(6): 32–38.

Peterson, Shira M., and Lucia French. 2008. "Supporting Young Children's Explanations through Inquiry Science in Preschool." *Early Childhood Research Quarterly* 23(3): 395–408.

Pica, Rae. 2009. *Jump into Science: Active Learning for Preschool Children.* Beltsville, MD: Gryphon House.

Sackes, Mesut, Kathy C. Trundle, and Lucia M. Flevares. 2009. "Using Children's Books to Teach Inquiry Skills." *Young Children* 64(6): 24–26.

Sackes, Mesut, Kathy C. Trundle, and Lucia M. Flevares. 2009. "Using Children's Literature to Teach Standard-Based Science Concepts in the Early Years." *Early Childhood Education Journal* 36(5): 415–22.

Samarapungavan, Ala, Panayota Mantzicopoulos, and Helen Patrick. 2008. "Learning Science through Inquiry in Kindergarten." *Science Education* 92(5): 868–908.

Satterlee, Donna J., and Grace D. Cormons. 2008. "Sparking Interest in Nature—Family Style." *Young Children* 63(1): 16–20.

Shaffer, Lauren F., Ellen Hall, and Mary Lynch. 2009. "Toddlers' Scientific Explorations: Encounters with Insects." *Young Children* 64(6): 18–23.

Shepardson, Daniel P. 2002. "Bugs, Butterflies, and Spiders: Children's Understandings about Insects." *International Journal of Science Education* 24(6): 627–43.

Spangler, Steve. 2009. "Beyond the Fizz: Getting Children Excited about Doing Real Science." *Young Children* 64(4): 62–64.

Starbuck, Sara, and Maria Olthof. 2008. "Involving Families and Communities through Gardening." *Young Children* 63(5): 74–79.

Stoddart, Trish, America Pinal, Marcia Latzke, and Dana Canaday. 2002. "Integrating Inquiry Science and Language Development for English Language Learners." *Journal of Research in Science Teaching* 39(8): 664–87.

Torquati, Julia, and Jana Barber. 2005. "Dancing with Trees: Infants and Toddlers in the Garden." *Young Children* 60(3): 40–47.

Trundle, Kathy C., and Mesut Sackes. 2008. "Sky Observations by the Book: Lessons for Teaching Young Children Astronomy Concepts with Picture Books." *Science and Children* 46(1): 36–39.

West, Martha. 2007. "Problem Solving: A Sensible Approach to Children's Science and Social Studies Learning—and Beyond." *Young Children* 62(5): 34–41.

Williams, Alyson E. 2008. "Exploring the Natural World with Infants and Toddlers in an Urban Setting." *Young Children* 63(1): 22–25.

Index

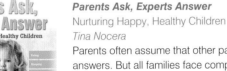
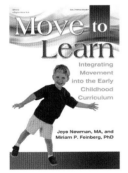
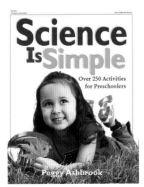

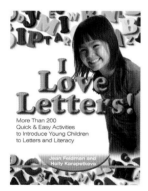
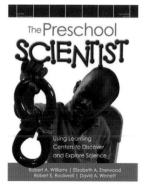